RUN

BELIEVE, BEHOLD, BECOME

HEATHER BAXTER

with Rebecca Gumina

Run Your Race!

Heather Baxter

2020

WESTBOW·
PRESS
A DIVISION OF THOMAS NELSON
& ZONDERVAN

WestBow Press books may be ordered through booksellers or by contacting:

WestBow Press
A Division of Thomas Nelson & Zondervan
1663 Liberty Drive
Bloomington, IN 47403
www.westbowpress.com
1 (866) 928-1240

ISBN: 978-1-4908-7756-3 (sc)
ISBN: 978-1-4908-7755-6 (e)

Library of Congress Control Number: 2015906510

Print information available on the last page.

WestBow Press rev. date: 06/30/2015

With all my heart,

I would like to say thank you to my mother-in-law, Chris.

She became my first mentor long before I even desired to show up at the starting line to Run my own Race. She helped me see God's will in the middle of miles 5, 10, 12, 18, and 20. Those hard miles became spiritual markers that opened the door for God's presence to reach me through others in my life (you know who you are: thank you, thank you!)

Chris: Thank you for teaching me that God sees us at the end of the Race, and that His vision goes beyond our circumstances.

Thank you for pushing me to allow God to

heal my marriage,

cleanse my soul,

and give me eyes to see His dreams for my life.

And therefore, Mom, I dedicate this book to you.

CONTENTS

ABOUT THE STUDY

*"BEHOLD, I am with you and will keep you wherever you
go! And I will bring you back to this land, for I will not leave
you until I have done what I have spoken to you."*
(Genesis 28:15)

How awesome is this? God has placed us in this land – in other words, this *Race* –
and He has determined that we will win!

Wherever you may be, whether struggling or celebrating, there is always a
leg of God's Race waiting for you. With the strength of the Lord, we are to walk
toward that Starting Line and allow God's truths in this study to empower us
to embrace the full Race, to keep pressing on, and to be reassured that all the
while, He is building our character, faith, and strength with each and every step.
We cannot Run perfectly, but we can certainly Run the Race marked out for us,
and finish well. Let's *Run in Such a Way.*

Run is designed for both interactive personal study and group discussion. The
seven weeks of this study will meet you in whichever lane you are standing in: it
does not matter how fast you are, how long you have been Running, or how far
you think you can go. As long as you are moving toward the Prize, you will be
discovering, and recovering, all God has for you. Running can be contagious.
The inspiration and motivation among Runners can be just what is needed to
push through that extra mile … and so we do this as a Running *community*. Do
the homework. Commit to group time. Allow the weekly teaching to spur you
toward the Finish Line.

Each week's cover page will carry the study's theme Bible verse. Don't skip over
our theme Bible verse: say it, write it, meditate on it … and by the end, you just
may have memorized it! Toward that end, there will be regular opportunities for
you to write it out. Each week's work will begin with an overall "Warm Up" page,

followed by five days of homework, with the last day's assignment prompting you to evaluate your pace, talk about it with your Trainer, and give thanks for the chance at joy. Along the way, there will be testimonies called "Mile Markers" and some "Strength Training Tips," and at the end of each week, there will be the option of pushing a little harder; this is called the "Extra Lap."

A few more comments:

- All Bible verses are from the NIV translation, unless otherwise noted.
- If a significant word is capitalized, we intend for that to indicate a *spiritual interpretation*. Example: "race" is a human footrace; "Race" refers to your spiritual journey.

We are so excited to Run alongside you as the soles of our feet tread upon scripture together. We pray that the miles we log together will become a spiritual marker in your life. We have struggled, and still struggle, with particular miles in our Races, and each week we will take a rest stop together, and we'll fill you in while we catch our collective breath! Our physical and spiritual muscles still knot up, *but* God will continue to create in all of us a faithful *Runner*.

LEADER'S GUIDE

Suggestions for Leaders:

These brief instructions will help you lead an effective Bible study. Many times we only have about 60 minutes to finish our group time together. I would like to suggest some of the main components to go over in group time for each session. Please encourage the ladies to complete each lesson before meeting. I suggest for the sake of time that you zoom in on this Leader Guide's "highlights and hints" area for each week's session. Don't feel you have to complete every session, Day 1 through Day 5. The goal of this study is for each participant to dig deep with scripture and themes all week long and apply their findings to their lives. At each group meeting you will discuss your experiences in certain areas.

Creating social media groups or hashtags is a great way to keep the energy moving and stirring for the duration of the study. Consider talking with your ministry team to create this space!

My suggestion is for an eight-week Bible study with two-hour sessions.

The first week is an introduction, and the last week (week 8) is session 7. Session 7 is shorter to allow for a nice review time for all material.

Flow of a morning or evening session:

* Coffee and fellowship time, 15 minutes
* Teaching leader presents a lesson on the content of the material, 45 minutes (Teaching videos will be available soon for this study!)

* Discussion time in small groups and prayer, 60 minutes

A few hints for group leaders for the overall material and layout of the study before I break down each session:

* Always read the warm-ups before each session; this breaks us in/stretches us and sets the stage for the session.
* Encourage the ladies to memorize the Key Verse, 1 Corinthians 9:24–27. Make some fun index cards with the verse on each to pass out on the first day. Encourage the ladies to keep their cards in a prominent place throughout the week.
* Encourage the ladies to treat this study like a personal journal. Mark it up! Highlight and have fun; make studying and learning pretty.

HINTS AND HIGHLIGHTS:

Introductory session/Week 1

A small lesson taught by a teaching leader to charge and encourage the ladies, followed by their first group time. In the first group session, discuss the flow of the material and go over the style of the book study. Touch your books and look at the setup together. Share and explain. For example, each session consists of five days, with the fifth being a review. Explain to the group that they can get through all the material in one week if they generate a daily quiet/study time. Help them generate a plan. Also highlight the Mile Markers and Extra Miles located in each session.

Do the Ice Breaker called "Breaking in our shoes together" and then review the introductory material. Please try to start Session 1/Warmup and Day 1 together.

Session 1: A Runner

Start with a quick review of Day 2 on the training tips, and then apply these to Day 3 and Day 4.

Be sure to leave time in Session 1 to do the Extra Mile lesson together as a group. Located on pages 37–40, this is a great place to stretch and get ready to Run!

Session 2: Why Run?

Day 1: "Hope will chase you down" is the same as the Extra Mile on page 74–78

This lesson is to help participants map out their personal faith stories. Have them use the scriptures and this lesson to teach them how to see God working in their personal Races. I suggest you have them do the Extra Mile and then go around and share stories. Encourage participants to focus on the Day 1 lesson during the week so they can map out their stories in the Extra Mile for that session. I use my personal story as an example in the Extra Mile lesson!

Day 2: Ask the group which stage each person feels like they are currently in and how that stage is shaping or has shaped them. It is important to do the work ahead of time. This is a fun lesson; we see our lives in the creation stages of a butterfly! *"Without change, there would be no butterflies."*

Day 3: This is another lesson on stages. Again, ask each member which stage spoke to their current Races and why.

Day 4: Do the questions on the pages and then ask members to share "highlighter" moments for that session. Take time to pull some of those verses and questions out.

Session 3: Run with Tenacity

Pull from each lesson, but pay particular attention to Day 3 and Day 4. These two lessons will help participants learn to dream big and prepare for the teaching of how to journal in this session's Extra Mile.

Prepare for next week:

Bring a sleeve of saltine crackers for next week's lesson. If this is not done during the teaching lesson as a whole group before small break-out groups, I suggest taking the fun, two-minute challenge explained in the Extra Mile of session 4. Fun and laughter are always good in groups.

Session 4: Runner's Roadblocks

Day 3: *sensitive material* – but I encourage this lesson for sure.

The Extra Lap has a fun activity. Ask for two volunteers to do the activity, and then do the lesson that follows. This will have the group laughing after discussing the sensitive material from Day 3.

Session 5: All In

All of Day 1, Day 3, and Day 4. (Really stay focused this week; there is a lot of work to highlight and review.)

Session 6: A Winner!

Day 3 will be a great teaching lesson, so I encourage you to discuss the crowns, and which crowns your group members feel they may be rewarded and why. This session is very important. Many do not realize we are given rewards based on how we Run in life! Do not miss this lesson!

Day 4 is short, but it is very important to end strong with this lesson.

Session 7

This is a very short lesson. Please go over together the example/lesson of how to "pray the lanes" at your local running/walking track. This is a great activity to help you get through your prayers while walking or running.

After that lesson please use this time to wrap up and pick a few favorite lessons from all sessions. Have participants share about how the lessons have trained them to Run better and in ways that are pleasing to God.

Also, please challenge the ladies to share if they memorized the key verse!

I pray you enjoy this study; it's a real blessing to Run beside everyone.

ABOUT THE AUTHORS

Running helped rid me of guilt and the need to control others.

Running knocked down the rules and regulations of religion and gave me Relationship.

Running gave me a fresh start by helping me let go of all my mistakes.

Running reminds me that life is intimate and not supposed to be continually full of programmed activity and layers of commitments.

Running allows me to *change* and develop new habits.

Running allows me to see my life in a new light, from God's point of view.

And now I desire to *chase* after all that God has for me!

I am an ordinary gal desiring to live an extraordinary life in Christ.

HEATHER BAXTER holds a bachelor's degree from Central Michigan University and previously worked in the mental health field as a licensed therapeutic specialist. Once God got ahold of her heart, she experienced a life-changing turn that had her Running in a new direction.

She has church staff experience in women's ministry, and has led Bible studies, retreats and conferences. Heather became an ordained minister in February 2011, and continues to further her education while using her gifts and energies and passions to Run alongside other women in this Race. She frequently participates in regional races, and in 2012 ran her first full marathon in Chicago.

Heather is married to Dan Baxter. She credits him with teaching her how to run her first mile – and for running right alongside her as she completed her first marathon. They live in Livonia, Michigan with their three children (Benjamin, Brittni, and Alivia), a chocolate lab, and two teacup Chihuahuas. NorthRidge Church in Plymouth, Michigan is their home church and where God has called them to serve, love, and Run. On pages 74–75, 119, 145 and 184–185 you can find specific mile marker moments that shaped Heather's story.

Let's get connected!
Facebook: Heather Baxter
Twitter: @heatherBxt
Instagram: HeatherBaxter1
Email: Heather@hbministries.com

~~~~~~

REBECCA GUMINA prefers to walk.

She has a bachelor's degree in communications and some seminary work experience. She is a licensed minister and was an associate pastor at her church in Ohio, and like associate pastors everywhere, her responsibilities included Bible teaching, music ministry, youth, women's ministry, bulletin proofreading, and making sure the furnace always kicked on in time for January Sunday services. Prior to that, Rebecca was a professional journalist in print and television media for nearly 20 years. She married John 30 years ago, has two daughters and two sons, a son-in-law, a new grandson, three cats, and a turtle. She and her family live in Northville, Michigan and are members of NorthRidge Church.

~~~~~~

The idea for *Run* dropped into Heather's heart during, well, a run ... and a year of work later, Heather had the makings of a Bible study. Enter Rebecca, who loved fine sentences, proper grammar, and all things punctuation. Or, as we like to say: Heather brought the recipe and the ingredients, and Rebecca peeled, diced, spiced, and set it to simmer.

We hope you are nourished by our stew.

~~~~~~

IVA SOPIC, our illustrator, has a B.A. in graphic arts from Wayne State University, Detroit, MI.

SESSION ONE: LECTURE NOTES

GROUP DISCUSSION/ICE BREAKER

Running Mates: Breaking in our Shoes Together

Let's take a few minutes and examine ourselves. Which of the following best describes how you tend to relate to the word *Run?* Share your responses with your Running Mates.

- I'm *ready* to face life and Run straight forward.
- I am running from my pain, pressure, past.
- My mascara runs faster than I do.
- I am running on fumes.
- I go running only when I have to: the ice cream truck is doing 60 …
- If found on the ground, please drag to the Finish Line.
- It's a hill: get over it! (I may be impatient with others who don't Run like me.)
- I have worn glass slippers my whole life, but am ready for Running Shoes.
- My feet hurt.
- I am nervous … but I need to make myself stronger than my excuses.
- I used to Run. I don't know why I stopped.
- I don't Run because …
- I find Running boring.
- I Run … in circles. Why can I not seem to progress?
- I Run slowly.
- I am fast and furious and wear myself out. I need to pace myself.

1. Are you a physical runner? If so, how long have you been running, and what has been your longest distance?

2. Are you a spiritual Runner? If so, do you have a marked moment when you know you turned your Race over to God? Or have you stumbled off trail, and then found your footing again?

SESSION ONE

A Runner

1 CORINTHIANS 9: 24-27

Do you not know that in a race all the runners run, but only one gets the prize? Run in such a way as to get the prize. Everyone who is going to compete in the games goes into strict training. They do it to get a crown that will not last, but we do it to get a crown that will last forever. "Therefore, I do not run like a man running aimlessly; I do not fight like a man beating the air. No, I beat my body and make it my slave so that after I have preached to others, I myself will not be disqualified for the prize." (1 Corinthians 9:26–27)

SESSION ONE: A RUNNER

The Warm-up (Introduction to this Session)

The Bible is full of images that will help us to understand doing life with God. One of the most famous analogies is when the apostle Paul compared himself to a runner. The image of running is not only a personal favorite, but you will see that it is full of great parallels to our walk with Christ. I encourage you to think outside the box throughout the study, and grab ahold of the heart of a runner. In each session, the content will spell out the parallels. Grab hold of God's truth, put one foot in front of the other, and gain momentum.

Paul writes, "I have finished the race …" (2 Timothy 4:7) The word he used for "race" described an event with *obstacles* in it; it is actually more like getting through an obstacle course than a flat-out run. Paul himself went through many hurdles and obstacles in his life, and he completed his Race. I hope you can see that Paul is using a wonderful metaphor by comparing the Christian Race (life) to a footrace. He was one of the most disciplined Runners throughout Scripture, and he will teach us how to press on toward the mark for the Prize of the high calling of God in Christ Jesus.

In Philippians 3, Paul likens our faith and spiritual growth to the athlete who trains hard for the game. Paul understood that he had a Race to Run and goals to reach. He speaks to us of how pressing toward Jesus is the most important Race of our lives, and that it is upon us to be the best Runners we can possibly be. Many of us in the Christian life are *not* pressing on – we are not even *trying* to Run, and may have already pulled ourselves out of the Race, content to merely exist in this life, and maybe (yawn) have a seat. Some are not even interested in Running at all.

We *are* called to Train, to work out our faith, to not let spiritual idleness sideline us – but to Run and Focus like the seasoned Athletes we were created to become.

To really understand Paul's imagery of runners in a race, let's look at the culture of sports and running in the time period in which he lived. In the ancient city of Rome, there was a place called "Campus." It was a large section of plains by the Tiber River used originally as a drill and training ground for soldiers. In time, Campus became ancient Rome's track and field. All over the region, men practiced hard at racing, jumping, boxing, and more. Ancient sports and competition were very important, and winning was all that mattered. There were no second or third places – no silver or bronze. Victory (*"nike"*) was the ultimate goal of every athlete. And the only goal. This may have inspired Paul's words when he wrote, "runners in a race all run, but only *one* will receive the prize."

The ancient runners didn't participate because it was fun or convenient. They would run to achieve excellence – to become all they were capable of being. In the days ahead, we will study how to Run to achieve excellence in our own lives, and learn what our unique Races look like. Paul teaches us that this is not a mere game; it is life or death. It's not going to be easy, but we will learn how to set a goal, understand the Finish Line, and embrace the concept of true Winning.

There *are* rules of Training, and we will study them. To the Corinthians, Paul explained these rules, saying that that no one wins the victory crown unless they compete according to the rules. In the ancient Olympic games, the rules governed not only the race itself, but also all the preparation leading up to the competition. So by all means, let's pull out the Training Manual and make sure we get these rules right.

The rest of our lives stretch before us. Sure, we are called, occasionally, to sprint. But most of our Running will be the long slog in the rain and shine, putting one foot intentionally in front of the other, whether that foot lands in a puddle or a meadow. We are after the satisfying conclusion of the long course, the marathon, finishing *well*.

You *are* a Runner! If you don't yet believe that, take God's word for it. Lace up, girlfriends!

On your mark … get set … GO!

SESSION ONE: A RUNNER

Day One "The Starting Line"

The Starting Line is just that – a place to start Running! Ladies, it does not matter what you look like, how much or how little prepared you feel, how in shape you feel or how decked out you are in cute shoes. It does not matter whether you can run to the mailbox or even around the block. At *this* Starting Line, all qualify!

On your mark

God has drawn the Starting Line for you to begin Running. It is the line on which you stand and gaze off into the distance and wonder what adventures lie ahead. From the moment you place your toes on the base of the line, He will begin work in your heart and life and complete it. He is the Author and the Finisher of your faith. (Hebrews 12: 1–2)

So, if this Starting Line is drawn by God, then the Race is probably *about* God, *for* God, and *toward* God. We beg your pardon if this comes across harshly, but we need to make something very clear from the get-go: apart from faith in Christ, you are not even in the right Race event. (If you are not sure you have crossed the line into faith in Jesus, please contact your small group leader, and she will help you understand this.)

Are you on the sidelines of God's Race?
Are you trying to Run a Race designed by yourself?
Are you living according to the deceit of the mighty *me*?

In a running event, you wear timing chips on your shoes. Your time does not "activate" until you cross the starting line mat – and it is by those turned-on sensors that your race is run and timed and marked. Our relationship with Christ is activated in the same way: once we become believers, the Holy Spirit is set up within us. The Spirit will help you learn to grow and Run in such a way. There will be times when you'll want to slow to a jog, but the Spirit will prod you to resume your pace. When you start to veer of your path, the Spirit will pull you back on. If you try to sit down and sit out the Race, the Spirit just may pull the chair out from under you. Oh, yes He will! And then He'll extend His hand, pull you up off your bum, and set your feet right and to Running once again.

You see, the Holy Spirit – your Race "sensor" – is also your biggest cheerleader and encourager! Running strong means Running *in* the Spirit so that you can Run the Race with confidence in such a way, and Run with perseverance because you are drawing from the core strength of Almighty God through the Holy Spirit. Yup. That is a big run-on sentence that means: the Spirit as Runner's Fuel, and the Spirit as a Personal Trainer.

Let's Fuel up and Train.

"Results are based on use, in conjunction with training"

We often see this statement, or something like it, written on some brand of energy supplement. It is intended for sustained performance, optimal delivery, and increased hydration and blood circulation to the body. The same concept exists for the spiritual Runner: the energy/fuel of God the Spirit enables the Christ follower to Run harder and desire God's *Race* for their lives.

Look up John 14:26 and write it below.

Look up 1 Corinthians 2:13 and write it below.

And now, write out 2 Corinthians 12: 8–10. _____

Set aside a few minutes and thank God for the Race He has marked out for you. Ask Him for eyes to see the path clearly and for the strength to stay in your lane. Ask Him for ears to hear His Training and for ever-present awareness of your need for His Fuel.

Get set

In that last verse you wrote out in 2 Corinthians, Paul spoke of thorns in his flesh and how God's grace was sufficient to see him through his Race anyway. In his own weakness, in hardships and persecutions, he would boast gladly because then it was clear that Christ's power was at work. Thorns are circumstances beyond our control that God allows in order to grow us.

But Paul didn't talk about pebbles in his shoes. There is a difference between pebbles and thorns.

Pebbles are things that we allow to come with us on the Run, but that don't belong there. Pebbles are things that we invite to hurt and hamper or slow and stop us. We get so accustomed to having them with us that we even forget they are tagging along for the ride, until our feet hit the ground, and *ouch*. How'd that get in there? Oh, yeah … we bring it everywhere, even though it doesn't belong in our shoes or on our journeys. Pebbles such as …

"Am I good enough?"
"I should have started a long time ago …"
"My past is too heavy to carry. I am weighed down."
"I have failed so many times at this one turn of the track."
"I've always been ridiculed for my 'latest' jump into something. What makes me think this will be any different?"

That self-talk might be enough to keep our feet frozen in place, *except for the fact that*, in Christ, we are new creations; we were set apart before time began; we are a people chosen by an Almighty God.

The first mention of Saul (later, "Paul") is in the book of Acts, when he is introduced after the stoning of Stephen as the "persecutor." Stephen would be the first Christian martyr (illegally murdered by an enraged mob), and Saul would become known for his blood thirst. He hunted down Christians. And he wore the thrill of the hunt like a mantel.

Then came Jesus on the Damascus Road (Acts 9), and Saul found his Starting Line.

"But the Lord said ... '...this man is My chosen instrument to take My name to Gentiles, kings, and..."

At the piercing of Heaven's light into world history, Saul became a new creation on a new Race, with a new name and a call on his life that set him apart from all others. Christ Jesus did that for Saul-turned-Paul, and He loves you no less.

Jesus will do that for you, too.
Even if there is a thorn you bear, shake out the pebbles.
In faith, place your feet in the ready posture ... get set.
(You are about to *go*.)

He's got this.

We will learn from Paul throughout this study, as his Race has much to teach us. God has reached out to humankind with a loving Race Plan for each of us – a plan that is set apart from all the world has to offer.

Look up Galatians 1:15–17 and write it below.

When Paul was called by grace to *go*, did he consult anyone or run it past his best friend? Did he fly off to weigh the opinions of others? Did he stop to reconsider the past pebbles and wonder if he was a new creation?

Or did he place his feet in the ready posture, get set, and *go*?
Yes, he did. Even immediately.

GO!

Every Runner's story is different, but the Starting Line is the same:
God *chose* you, and calls you to faith.
He will give you a unique Race to Run.
As you log the miles, the Lord will set you apart more and more, and your path will become clearer.
What do you think your response should be?

> "I'm going to *Run* this Race, and finish, and obtain the Prize!"
> "I'm not going to live my whole life missing out on what God has for me – *what God has picked out* just *for me!*"
> "I am not going to 'settle' … instead, I want the sweat on my brow, the ache of growing new muscles, and the exhilaration of tearing over the Finish Line in victory!"

We have a shared destiny: A Finished Life.
…The Race is not to the swift, or the battle to the strong**,** *or bread to the wise, or riches to the discerning, or favor to the skillful; rather, time and chance happen to all of them.* (Ecclesiastes 9:11)
Make the most of your God-appointed opportunity. Thank Him for your life. Open yourself to His Training.
Run.

TRAINING TIP …

In light of our shared destiny, picture yourself at the end of your Race – the end of your life. Now, look back on yourself where you are right now.
How would you encourage yourself? What words would you say?

SESSION ONE: A RUNNER

Day Two "Prepare to Succeed"

> …Train *yourself to be godly. For physical training is of*
> *some value, but godliness has value for all things, holding*
> *promise for both the present life and the life to come.*
> *(1 Timothy 4: 7b–8)*

Paul uses the example of physical exercise and training to illustrate a great spiritual truth.

The Greeks put much importance on bodily exercises because an athletic event was of great importance to them. The parallel is clear: Christians should put as much effort into spiritual Training as athletes put into physical preparation.

The runner trains to build strength, endurance, and power.

No one runs a marathon the first time they put foot to pavement. Building strength, endurance, and power happens over time and with intentional training toward that one goal. The same idea translates to the spiritual Race. God does not expect us to know everything, sense everything, and obey everything all at once and get it right immediately. We are all works in progress! By the same measurement, growth in strength, endurance, and power will not happen by accident. It takes intentional, consistent effort over time.

What follows is a set of weekly Training goals. I encourage you to embrace each session and day's homework with these goals in mind. Here's the truth: focus on these goals and implement them into your life … and *something will* happen. God will honor your heart and your commitment. His response to you will be as unique as your fingerprints, but He will respond.

Training goals:

1. Spend quiet time with your Coach (God).

    Quiet time is a time of prayer, Bible study, or meditation in the presence of God. Day Five of each session will provide a suggested structure and guidance.

    Put a checklist together on your calendar or to-do list and plan for this quiet time.

2. Run on the Word and Promises of God.

    Learn to Run in agreement with the Word you believe each day: Read and examine the scriptures for each week's session. Memorize scripture. This study we will be chewing on is I Corinthians 9:24–27: write it on an index card and carry it with you, or post it in the bathroom or on the visor of your car. Say it out loud over and over again – repetition brings memory. Record it each week on Day 5.

3. Run in prayer.

4. Train with a Team.

    Being part of a small group or community of believers is helpful to your spiritual growth.

    Proverbs 27:17 says, "As iron sharpens iron, so one person sharpens another." We need to lean into each other because we happen to share one Body! As the Body of Christ, we need all our parts functioning. Besides, Training together makes the Run easier.

5. Share your story with someone.

    Talk easily and conversationally about what you're up to. Help those around you see their lives – their Races – from God's perspective. On

Day 5 each week, you will be presented with a sharing challenge from a specific passage of truth that you learned that week. Take the challenge.

6. Set a goal and write it down.

Put it on paper, and learn to press into a Big, Strong, Audacious Goal – whether it is for the day, the week, or the year.

Now, on to today's lesson: Preparing to Succeed!

Perhaps you are standing at the Starting Line today, really wanting to Run, but your insides are in knots: "Doesn't Training mean pain? Isn't there suffering involved in Working It Out? I was kind of hoping I'd signed up for a Fun Run!"

The bad news is that suffering and success go hand in hand.

The good news is that suffering and success go hand in hand.

Yes, hardships happen to the righteous, and life's difficulties may collide with our Races, and that is the reality of this earthly existence. We also have an Enemy, the father of lies, who will stick an ugly foot out into our paths just to see us trip and fall. Satan wants to mess up your Race and bring confusion into your life because he wants to keep you as far from the Finish Line as he can. So, cue the weary muscles, the heavy feet, the procrastination, the discouragement, the flirty thoughts of just giving up.

As I sit here writing these words, I can see in my mind's eye a handful of my friends who are Running their Races amidst a great deal of suffering. I know that they are hanging on by a thread … pushing with gritted teeth through the hardest miles of their journeys. But they Run. And they proclaim Romans 8:18 … "I consider that my present sufferings are not worth comparing with the glory that will be revealed in me."

Let's consider one of David's hardest miles: I Samuel 22.

At this point in David's story, he had a string of impressive battlefield successes and had been an assistant to the king, but was now enduring considerable suffering at the hands of his best friend's father, Saul, the King of Israel. Saul, in a rage of jealousy and insecurity, was hunting David down to kill him, and to protect himself and his family, David was now a fugitive. He was on the run, afraid for his life, and hurt and confused by the turn of events. (See I Samuel 20.)

He'd gone from stunning success to life-threatening suffering in a quick reversal of fortune. And yet, scripture assures us that in the midst of his crisis, David continually turned to the Lord and trusted Him.

I Samuel 22:1 tells us that David escaped to the *Cave of Adullam*. "Adullam" means *refuge*, and some believe the cave was located in the valley of Elah. But it wasn't the cave that was David's true refuge – Almighty God was! Here's the kicker about the valley of Elah: this was the same valley where David had won his fight against Goliath all those years and battles ago. That victory had been a launching pad – David's Starting Line – in learning to trust God in the face of unimaginable odds. You see, my friend, Valleys and Victories are part of life and often intertwined. And here in the cave, exhausted, David looked around at the familiar landscape and was reminded of God's Plan and sovereignty.

I cry aloud to the LORD; I lift up my voice to the LORD for mercy.
I pour out my complaint before him; before him I tell my trouble.
When my spirit grows faint within me, it is you who know my way.
In the path where I walk, men have hidden a snare for me.
Look to my right and see; no one is concerned for me. I have no refuge; no one cares for my life.
(Psalm 142:1–4)

Have mercy on me, O God, have mercy on me, for in you my soul takes refuge.
I will take refuge in the shadow of your wings until the disaster has passed. I cry out to God Most High, to God, who fulfills his purpose for me. He sends from heaven and saves me, rebuking those who hotly pursue me; God sends his love and his faithfulness.

My heart is steadfast, O God; I will sing and make music. Awake my soul! …
I will praise you, O Lord, among the nations; I will sing of you among the peoples. For great is your love, reaching to the heavens; your faithfulness reaches to the skies. Be exalted, O God, above the heavens; let your glory be over all the earth.
(Psalm 57:1–3, 7–11)

A tale of two Psalms

David wrote both of the above Psalms while in the cave on the run from Saul. These give us great cave lessons.

In the Bible, a Psalm will often have a subtitle under its numerical reference that gives us a historical explanation ("when he was in the cave"), a distinction between song and prayer ("a prayer"), or a clue to authorship and purpose. In this case, Psalm 142 is a *maskil* of David.

The word *maskil* means "instruction, for understanding." While in the cave, and in this Psalm 142 prayer, David was praying for instruction and understanding. Read the passages again. Do you hear his cry? A cave experience is one from which you desperately want to escape, but while you are in the midst of it, you are drawing close to God. In the Cave of Adullam, David was running from Saul, but was also turning to Run toward God. He had stopped running *from*, and begun Running *to*. God's victory was near.

By the time David penned Psalm 57 (The Psalms are not in chronological order), he was clearly growing more hopeful and confident. He was learning to Run in Such a Way! In fact, by the time Psalm 57 was numbered and collected among the other worship writings for the Book of Psalms, David was putting this Psalm to *song*! Here's a kicker: the Psalm is indicated to be set to the tune of "Do Not Destroy." Don't you love that the Israelites had a tune by that name? And that they kept adding new verses as God delivered them yet again?

Cave lessons

Let's learn a few things from David's cave experience. How did he stay in his Race?

1. David chose to *trust* God.

   Re-read the first few verses of Psalm 57. David had nowhere else to turn but towards God, and this is what would bring success *within* the suffering. While you are in your cave, God will come to where you are and confirm His faithfulness and His promises to you – God will use your cave as a banner to write His love over your life!

14

How can Psalm 57:1 speak into your life? Write out the verse here, and instead of the word "disaster," *name* the troubling circumstance in your life, and then pray the verse.

2. David chose to *turn* his life and situation over to God.

   David revealed his confidence in God. He shared how God was faithful, and expressed so much trust through his words. Beginning in verse 7, we hear words such as, "My heart is steadfast," "I will sing," and "Awake, my soul!" He had intentionality in the *turn* and in telling his feelings of what was what! He was declaring to himself the truth. Without reminding ourselves of truth, our feelings can overwhelm us and our Races can come to a screeching, fearful stop.

Look up I Peter 4:19 and write it below.

   There are two action steps in this passage for what to do within the suffering. Apply them below to your "disaster."

   Commit:

   Continue to do good:

3. David chose *togetherness*.

If we dip back into I Samuel 22, you will see that after David arrived at the Cave of Adullam, word got back to his family that he was there, *and they came to him. And they stayed with him.*

> *When his brothers and his father's household heard about it, they* went down to him *there. All those who were in distress or in debt or discontented* gathered around him, *and he became their commander. About 400 men were with him. From there David went to Mizpah in Moab and said to the king of Moab, "Would you let my father and mother come and stay with you until I learn what God will do for me?" So he left them with the kind of Moab, and* they stayed with him as long as David was in the stronghold." *(I Samuel 22:1b–4) (Emphasis added.)*

Look back at the I Samuel 22 passage. Who joined David? His family, certainly. But then here came the rest: those in distress, discontentment, and debt. Hardly the happy-clappy among us, right? They were suffering together, but together, reminded one another of who God *was*. And then together, they made the turn to Trust. And together, witnessed the safety and provision of God, and God's victory over their circumstances. And *together*, they tell this story of their deliverance, their suffering becoming success, their testimony of God, thousands of years later.

> *And let us not neglect our meeting together, as some people do, but encourage and warn each other, especially now that the day of his coming back again is drawing near. (Hebrews 10:25 NLT)*

> *Rejoice with those who rejoice, and weep with those who weep. (Romans 12:15)*

Think of those in your life who are encouraging to you, especially when all you can see are cave walls.
Name them here: _____

Which parts of their encouragement do you like the most, and why? How does that feed you?

In what way can you emulate this kind of encouragement to someone else today? Write down a name and an action. Pray for them, and then follow through on your action step.

"I love the morning of a big race event because so many people from so many places gather at the starting gates. Masses of people head out, as one, to get into position to Run together. Being part of such a huge, excited, eager crowd really gets your Race juices going! You see, God recognized the importance of togetherness from the beginning of Creation with Adam and Eve. God continually encourages His people to come together to worship, serve, study, and fellowship. God knows we need the strength found in numbers, especially during our Cave Experiences."

SESSION ONE: A RUNNER

Day Three "Run Your Race"

Therefore, since we are surrounded by such a great cloud of witnesses, let us throw off everything that hinders and the sin that so easily entangles. And let us Run with perseverance the Race marked out for us, fixing our eyes on Jesus, the author and perfecter of our faith, who for the joy set before him endured the cross, scorning its shame, and sat down at the right hand of the throne of God. (Hebrews 12:1–2) (Emphasis added.)

Your life is a Race that God marked out for you.

What a challenging and captivating thought! God created every person to Run with *purpose*, not just beating the air and taking up space here on earth.

The Greek word for run is "dioko" (pronounced dee-O'ko). It means to run swiftly, as though trying to catch up, or catch someone or something – to run hard after.

I believe God has called us to learn *how to* Run in such a way as to pursue, seek eagerly after, and earnestly acquire all God has for our lives.

Look up Jeremiah 29:11 and write it below: _____

_____

From this verse, what are God's promises to you about your Race? _____

Look up Ephesians 3:20 and write it below: _____
_____

What is this verse promising you today about your Race? _____
_____

The Greek word for race *is "stadia." It is from this Greek root that we get our English word "stadium."*

Running the Race of faith puts us in the arena for all the spectators to watch! Whether we realize it or not, eyes are trained on us from the sidelines – and maybe even from a few lanes over – to watch *how* we choose to Run. Yes, we may fall and stumble at some point, but we were created to have a winner's heart and Run our best to the glory of God. Daily, we have the opportunity to influence the spectators in the arenas of our lives.

I remember watching a video of an athlete taking a terrible fall and stumbling hard during a 600-meter Big Ten championship race. She got up quickly, resumed her race, and went on to *win*! It was a stunning victory that garnered millions of hits on YouTube. (You can check it out yourself at: http://www.youtube.com/watch?v=uqnqLrakxY8.)

Her race was about her rise!

Would the victory have tasted so sweet – or would the victory have become so memorable – if she had run an ordinary race? Would the crowd have exploded so? When a fall becomes a victory, the fall itself is not only redeemed, but it becomes an integral and precious memory of the Race. The ability to pick themselves up and resume the race comes as a result of all athletes' training.

The Greek word for athlete *is "athlein" (derived from the word Athlos). An athlete was a person trained with one goal in mind: to compete in a contest and contend for a prize.*

Are *you* an athlete? Or do you know someone deeply committed to their training? Do you fully realize how many times they had to pull themselves out the door and go train … anyway? Whether they wanted to or not, whether it was raining or sunny, whether a hundred other things pulled on them, they saw to their training. Period.

It is the same when we Run for Christ. Many of us are hardly Training at all because we don't want to leave our comfort zones or be asked to stretch. The couch and the Fritos looking pretty appealing, and didn't I DVR my show? We battle the spiritual Run with the physical world tugging at us.

We need to get tougher spiritually and start Running. Following God's call is not taking a casual stroll in the park, looking forward to the potluck meal at the end. Strolling is fine sometimes. Potlucks are great! (Especially if the scalloped potatoes are extra cheesy.) But if we are called to Run hard after Jesus and activate all the promises of God in our lives, some of our strolls need to step it up into full-on Runs.

Look up Philippians 2:12 and write it below:

How does this verse speak to you? Especially the phrase "work out"? Explain in the space below.

If Running your Race was merely a matter of passive yield and surrender, then the Word of God would not point to countless truths about personal responsibility and obedience to your Training. If you showed up at a gym tomorrow and only stood and stared at the treadmill, it would do you no good at all. The structure, the directions, the equipment are all there waiting for you: you need to *climb on* and get to it.

What spiritual Training have you just been staring at? What Training might God be calling you to that you have spent months – years? – turning over in your head for consideration, rather than hopping on and getting to it already?

We can learn from the parallels between the training of athletes and the Training for the Race.

1. *Be consistent.*

Our Training must be consistent if we are to fulfill our potential. Paul brings out this idea of consistency in 2 Timothy 2:5: *"If anyone competes as an athlete, he does not receive the victor's crown unless he competes according to the rules."*

For the ancient Olympic Games, the rules governed not only the competition, but also the preparation. Athletes had to train rigorously for 10 months, or they were not allowed to compete for the prize. In training, there are rules. Respecting and adjusting our lives to the rulebook and applying the training consistently are what leads to victory.

In what areas do you need to become more consistent in your Race? _____

2. *Be disciplined.*

For training to reap its maximum benefits, an athlete must discipline her entire life, not just her time on the track. A well-trained athlete avoids distractions, eats well, gets sufficient rest, and avoids activities that could result in injury. In I Timothy, Paul encourages his "true son in the faith" to run away from the evil desires of youth and to, instead, pursue righteousness, faith, love, and peace. Review Hebrews 12:11 and answer the following questions:

Are you disciplining *all* parts of your life, so that you will grow in Christlikeness? _____

Remember that in Hebrews 12:1–2 we are told to throw off everything that hinders. What do you need to "throw off" in order to devote yourself to your Training?

_____

These questions will help you to start thinking about your personal Race and the changes that may need to follow. Take notes as you listen to others, and allow the Holy Spirit to guide you to the changes in your Running program. Remember: one step at a time! *Happy Running!*

***Fun Fact: The word "Gymnasium" comes from the Greek root "gymnos", meaning "nude". Athletes in the ancient Olympic Games would participate nude. Can we all shout a hallelujah that nude training is not part of our Training Manual?*

SESSION ONE: A RUNNER

Day Four "Running Hard"

*Fight the good fight of the faith. Take hold of the eternal
life to which you were called when you made your good
confession in the presence of many witnesses.
(1 Timothy 6:12)*

*But you, Timothy, man of God: Run for your life from all this. Pursue
a righteous life – a life of wonder, faith, love, steadiness, courtesy. Run
hard and fast in the faith. Seize the eternal life, the life you were called to,
the life you so fervently embraced in the presence of so many witnesses.
(1 Timothy 6:11-12) (MSG)*

Can you handle just one more Greek word for this week? Let's presume you've said yes! In the Greek, the word *fight* is a grittier, bloodier, more "duke-it-out" word than *squabble*.

The Greek *agonizomai* means to strive, fight or labor – literally to compete for a prize, to endeavor to accomplish something. So where's the blood? From the same root *agonizomai*, we derive our English words *agony* and *agonize*. There it is.

There is a struggle in every Christian's life. You can wriggle in God's grasp and struggle and stumble toward growth, but that's not the battlefield most of us land on. (After all, God already spilled His blood for you. The Christian "fight" is Good, because it has already been won by Jesus!)

The *agony* battle here on earth, in this lifetime, is the one between ourselves – and Satan's lies.

And this one's a doozy. There will come, in our Runs, many falls. Yesterday, we talked of how a Race can be defined by whether we Rise – and *how* we Rise – to continue. Your Run, Race, Fall, Rise, and Result will all be determined by which voice you are listening to, and which interpretation you choose. God has an end game, a goal, a *destiny* in mind for your life. Our Falls (flaws, mistakes, sin) do not disqualify us from the Race. The reverse is true! Interpreted correctly and biblically, our Falls mean we turn to Jesus to do life intimately with Him, to access the Holy Spirit's insight into our troubles, and to ask for God's power in our Races. This interpretation of events and ourselves brings us to real victory.

But then there is the voice that would translate your Fall unbiblically, even accusingly, and this is the one to which the flesh will run. Every. Stinkin'. Time.

So let's go with the first option, shall we? Let us choose Truth. Knowing who we are in Christ and how much we are loved will not keep us from unpleasant or difficult circumstances. Hardship is part of this earthly journey, but when we choose to use the Jesus translation of ourselves and our circumstances, we will indeed *rise above* and *take hold* of all He has for us. You are the *apple* of God's eye:

"Keep me as the apple of your eye; hide me in the shadow of your wings." (Psalm 17:2)

Maybe you do this, too:

When my girls were younger and we would have an apple as a snack, I would always cut the apple horizontally so that the seed pods within the apple took the shape of a perfect star! And I would say to them that on the inside of this fruit, God had designed a surprise to remind us of how much He loved us. We are the apple of His eye, and the point is that He wants us to shine like the stars He knows us to already be in Christ! May God prepare you to fully open your heart and mind to the unexpected.

God promises that when we choose to tuck in and snuggle up underneath the protection of His almighty wing, where it is safe and soft and true and forever, He will reveal to us a Race plan that is more, more, more than anything we could anticipate or expect.

Look up 1 Corinthians 2:9 and write it below.

How does this verse land on you today? What is your immediate reaction?

God's Race course for *you* is personal, *unique in all creation*, divinely purposed, and already written on your life. Take hold of this life to which you were called. Fight the agony that would pull you away. Believe the truth and Run in such a way that you attain the Prize God has for you.

Look up 1 Corinthians 9:24–27 and write it below. Yes, we have parked at this address before, and we are back again to drink deeply in a new way:

Direction + Correction, all under His Protection = Victory

Now go back up to the beginning of the verse, and highlight or underline the first four words.

Do you not know? This rhetorical question is a literary style Paul used to remind readers and listeners of what we should already know, but the repetition acts as an underscore with a bit of a push *to take hold of it* and take action accordingly.

Run to Win. In this passage of scripture, Paul gives the believers at Corinth an exhortation. It was not just an exhortation to run. It was an exhortation to run so that they would win and claim the victory Prize in any Race they submitted to God's authority.

Winning the spiritual Race is not dependent upon how fast you Run. It is determined by *how* you Run.

- You can Run in such a way that you are certain to lose.
- There is a right way, and a wrong way, to Run.
- Paul exhorted the Corinthians to Run to Win.

– He also told them how to do it.

The Bible is very practical in that way. It never gives you a command without also giving you the instruction and the resources to fulfill that command. It is the Christian's Training Manual, and it tells you how to Run the Race.

"Do you not know?" is found 10 times in this letter to the Corinthians. Read each of the following passages, and then jot down the main theme:

1 Corinthians 3:16 Don't you know that

1 Corinthians 5:6 Don't you know that

1 Corinthians 6:2 Don't you know that

1 Corinthians 6:3 Don't you know that

1 Corinthians 6:9 Don't you know that

1 Corinthians 6:15 Don't you know that

1 Corinthians 6:16 Don't you know that

1 Corinthians 6:19 Don't you know that

1 Corinthians 9:13 Don't you know that

1 Corinthians 9:24 (the verse we've been studying) Don't you know that

Paul was determined to communicate to the Corinthians the importance of God's authority in their lives. Christ requires a commitment that stirs us to embrace both risk and sacrifice. The phrase "Do you not know" uses a verb in Greek that is "perfect tense." This means the verb indicates something that happened in the past, *but the effects are current and the effects impact even the future!* This *matters.*

Our calling in Christ should motivate us to do whatever it takes to grow in Christ and live in obedience to Him.

In what areas in your life do you find difficult to obey the Lord, and why is it difficult? _____

Right now, how does your life glorify the Lord? What things do you do to honor Him? _____

The expectation of the Christian is that we are *in* the Race, and we are Running to win by applying great devotion, diligence, and discipline. And the energy to do that? We need to access all that is available to us through the Holy Spirit. *Ask* God to give you the mindset of giving Him your all. *Ask* God to show you what "Run in such a way" looks like in your life. *Ask* for counsel from wise and faithful mentors if you are struggling. *Ask* the Lord to help you understand in the coming weeks all that Paul was exhorting to the Corinthians.

Need a chore list to recall the You Version that's True? (Proclaim this out loud. Apply as needed!)

Do you not know that in him …

… I am alive with Christ! (Ephesians 2:5)
… I am free from the law of sin and death! (Romans 8:2)
… I am born of God and the evil one does not touch me! (1 John 5:18)
… I am holy without blame before Him in love! (Ephesians 1:4 and 1 Peter 1:16)
… I am complete in Him who is head of principality and power! (Colossians 2:10)

... I am the head and not the tail; I am above, and not beneath, because I pay attention to the commands of the Lord my God! (Deuteronomy 28:13)

... I am forgiven! (Ephesians 1:7)

TRAINING TIP: It is a *Mile Marker* when we can come to the place of contentment in our Runs and say "by the Grace of God, *I am what I am*, and His grace to me was not without effect. No, I worked harder than all of them – yet not I, but the grace of God that was with me." (1 Corinthians 15:10)

As I sit in Bible study small groups and listen to many share stories of hardship and mountain tops, it never fails that as women are engulfed into God's love and acceptance, they open up and share with honesty the Race courses they're currently Running. We learn that life is a journey, and together we will celebrate their stories in *Run*. What follows is the first of our "Mile Markers."

Mile Marker

Jennifer

There is nothing like the brisk morning air hitting your face as you step out into the running world. This has not always been a familiarity; in fact, *I hated running.* I hated that I had to give my time to something that was painful and took me away from my comforts in life. I had a secure little bubble that allowed me to avoid pain and people at all costs. Running would force me into muscle aches, blistered feet, and lost toenails, but it would force me to face my emotions and mental pain and frustrations with my past and how I was currently living my life. Without my knowing it was Him, God pressed me: "Jennifer, it's time to run."

So with six-year-old running shoes and just having had twins, I decided this was the time to get my life back and address the pain and frustration I had been hiding for so long.

My first frustration and pain: rape

As a teen I was very vulnerable and let my guard down to someone I thought was a friend. He raped me. The fear and hate after that began to reside in my heart: the fear of never finding a husband who would want someone who had been abused, and the hate for a God who had not protected me.

Second frustration: the death of my mom

On July 1, 2006 my mom died from a heart attack due to her Type I diabetes. I was only 23, and at that time in my life I still needed her. I was angry. She had been my best friend. It bothered me so much that God would take her away from me.

My final frustration: not being able to live a life of peace

Twins, financial strain, and job stresses all seemed to be pressuring my life, and I wanted to control the outcomes. God had a different plan. He wanted me to run.

Five weeks after the birth of my twin girls, I ran my first 5K. One year and five months after having the girls, I ran my first half marathon, and just one month after that, I ran my first marathon. My training for these events was accompanied by two amazing people. My running partners not only opened my eyes to running techniques and encouragement, but spiritual enlightenment as well. On our long runs, our talks centered around how amazing God was and how this was a sinful and painful world.

From our talks, I realized that I was so removed from my relationship with God that I was missing out on what He had truly given me: *Peace.*

Just as I realized I had peace from my busy life and from sadness, and the peace of knowing that God was in control, my running partners were struck with medical situations that hindered them from being able to run any longer. I felt, once again, stripped of the one thing that held me to God, but something was different now. I could still hear God impressing upon me.

One morning, I realized God had given me a wake-up call.

He showed me that life in this world was never safe and secure, but His love would *never* fail me. He had been right there during all my pains and frustrations and cried with me for all those years. He'd held me and known that down the road His plan for me was greater than I could ever imagine.

I still have ups and downs, but I can rest my head at
night, in peace, knowing that God is in control.
Currently, I still run. I have picked up two amazing little
running companions, my four-year-old girls!
My mission is to be a God-fearing mama and to teach and instill
in them the importance of what God can do in our lives. God
is good, and I continue to call on Him and praise His name
for all the blessings and trials that have come my way.

"Those who hope in the Lord will renew their strength. They will soar on wings like eagles; they will run and not grow weary, they will walk and not be faint."
(Isaiah 40:31)

SESSION ONE: A RUNNER

Day Five Personal Running Log

Pace yourself

Review the week's work: the scripture you have covered, the writings on the lines and in the margins. What would you ask God for this day? What did you not quite get this week? How can you serve Him more? Whom and what should you be praying for?

P Pray.
A Ask for God's vision for your life.
C Communicate back to God.
E Enter His Race for your life.

Run free in the space below: _____

Recovery questions

***What main thing did the study push me to *do*, *be*, or *feel* as a result of the material?

***What did God say to me through this week?

***How is my Run measuring up to this word? What action(s) will I take to bring my life in line with the word/message received this week?

My challenge

With what truth do I need to study and Train harder?

BLISTER:

"Ouch and Pinch": Jot down those moments this week that caused pain.

BLISS:

"Praise You and Thank You": Jot down your praises.

Team Spirit/Sharing Challenge: Think of someone you know who is limping right now. _____

Pray for them.

Look for an opportunity to share with them what you have learned this week.

Theme verse:

Do you not know that in a race all the runners run, but only one gets the prize? Run in such a way as to get the prize. Everyone who competes in the games goes into strict training. They do it to get a crown that will not last; but we do it to get a crown that will last forever. Therefore, I do not run like a man running aimlessly; I do not fight like a man beating the air. No, I beat my body and make it my slave so that after I have preached to others, I myself will not be disqualified for the prize. (1 Corinthians 9:24–27)

Write out the verses in the space below.

Pray the verses back to God, making them personal.

When you've memorized them, share *the verses by speaking them out loud to your small group! Great job!*

The Extra Lap

When we learn and desire to Run in such a way, the
Lord will begin to change our routes.
God wants to do something huge in your life. "Enlarge" means to
move, shift, and expand. It is not based on your ability. It is the Spirit
dwelling in you: all of the fullness of God that God wants to unleash
through your life. So it's not your ability − it's your expandability.
God needs expandable tents.
God uses elastic vessels that are able to change and grow with what God is doing.

Look at one of our favorite verses with me, Friends. We love the energy in this promise,
and we claim this for our lives. Please take this promise with you on your Run today.

"Enlarge the place of your tent, stretch your tent curtains wide, do not hold back.
lengthen your cords, strengthen your stakes.
For you will spread out to the right and to the left. Your descendants will
dispossess nations and settle in their desolate cities." (Isaiah 54:2–3)
(Emphasis added.)

I will share five points with you from this passage and
illustrate what it means to Run closer to Him.

1. ***"Enlarge/dream big mentality.*** The Truth teaches us to enlarge our
   tents. What does "tent" mean?

   The tent is a representation of a lifestyle of roaming from place to place
   aimlessly, frequently, or without a fixed pattern of movement. In ancient

times, and even today, this is the pattern for "pastoral nomads." Although in our culture and in this life we are prone to plant ourselves, physically, in one place for a time, we are also on a spiritual journey. Many times we Run aimlessly from place to place, when the better way is to aim at the Finish Line (eternity) and Run straight for *it.*

What is your vision of God and your (earthly) tent at this moment?

Expect great things from God! We have a mighty and great God, and although we say words about how God is the God of the impossible, we often don't live that way: we hole up, keep the flaps down, brace ourselves on our little plots of ground, and hope for the best. Or at least the "safest." God wants to *enlarge* so many things in our lives!

2. **Clear the ground. What do you usually do before you put up a tent in a particular spot?**

We need to clear the ground. We need to throw off that which hinders and so easily entangles – these words are very familiar by now, right? Look around you: what root stubs are yet protruding from the ground that you want to stake out? Is there debris scattered around? Dig out the stubborn roots, bag up the trash, and dispose of it properly. Clear and stake your ground.

What will you clear out this week?

3. **Stretch.** The passage explains the importance of stretching the curtains wide. Let's really look at this visual because it can be powerful. God wants us to be *open* to provisions and possibilities.

When something is stretched, it encounters pressure. It's the same with our faith Run. We will experience pain as we stretch. We might resist when under pressure, but as long as we endure, we will reap the fruit of our faith. We are reminded in this passage to try out new things, to move out of the box, to go beyond and live beyond what we can see. God is a God of possibilities. We may not understand all of what He will do in us and through us, but be sure of this: He has a plan and His rewards are amazing!

Think about what happens when you stretch the fabric of a tent to the stakes. There will be tension at every corner and every stake and in every pull as it is stretched.

    ---Allowing God to stretch us can mean we are stretched out of our comfort zones. What corners of your life/tent are being stretched right now?

    ---Stretching takes effort and sacrifice. You're not going to reach the stake and the anchor in the ground unless you're willing to pull – over the long haul, as the fabric adapts to the new length. And can we admit that it's often not a consistent, loving pull, but sometimes a hard yank? Life events will yank you toward that stretching, whether you agree to it or not.

    ---Stretching causes us to embrace discipline. Most of the pull *will* be through the daily commitment to the discipline of the Stretch: time with God, our Coach. Time in His Word, our Training Manual. The release of control to the Spirit's work in us. Every piece of us.

4. Lengthen/strengthen

When we enlarge and stretch out our territory, God wants us to keep our eyes fixed on Him, to hold onto His promises and find strength in His presence. He is reminding us to be both creative and careful. Our goal as we enlarge our boundaries is to glorify Him more. The cord and stake are used for strengthening things and keeping the tent up.

If a tent is kept in the same place, over time the tension releases and the tent gets droopy and saggy. This is when we need to tighten the ropes, or even pull out the stakes in the ground and tighten the cords – *reposition*. We pull them out of the ground, pull them out further from the tent, and then hammer the stakes deeper into the ground.

Many times in our Races, we will need to strengthen certain areas of our lives to keep our overall Runs strong and our tents taut. You know it's time when you feel your spirit is restless. When this unrest comes over you, don't cast about looking to point the finger at something or someone else. This unrest is a sign that your tent is sagging and you need to reposition your stakes.

This does *not* mean that you pull *out* of everything, or go to the other extreme and commit to every possible spiritual motivator, ministry, and service project available! But it can mean that you need to stand back and look at the sag prayerfully, and then ask God where and how He would have you reposition your stakes.

***Whatever your course, it is important that your tent stakes are hammered somewhere in God's Word, our Solid Ground. If your tent is sagging, the first question should be: "Am I anchored in His Word?" Without that grounding, our flesh will look for answers outside of Him in a heartbeat. So check that stake first, and then move on to the other corners of your tent.

5. **Expand.** God is promising us that we will spread to the right and to the left. He desires to bless and expand you for His glory because then the kingdom seeds also spread to the right and the left.

    This passage of scripture (Isaiah 54: 2–3) is a wonder-filled reminder that God wants us to Run in such a (fresh, new!) way.

God wants to *expand you*.

---**Expand** your worth in Christ. Below, write out a verse that explains your worth in God's eyes. (This week's homework provides plenty of examples … an apple, anyone?)

---**Expand** your identity beyond your circumstances. Remember David in the cave? Remind yourself how David handled his circumstances.

---**Expand** your knowledge of God. In what ways would you like to grow in this?

---**Expand** your God-implanted gifts and the call on your life. What steps can you take to reposition this particular stake?

SESSION TWO

Why Run?

1 CORINTHIANS 9: 24–27

Do you not know that in a Race all the runners run, but only one gets the prize? Run in such a way as to get the prize. Everyone who competes in the games goes into strict training. They do it to get a crown that will not last; but we do it to get a crown that will last forever. Therefore, I do not run like a man running aimlessly; I do not fight like a man beating the air. No, I beat my body and make it my slave so that after I have preached to others, I myself will not be disqualified for the prize.

SESSION TWO: LECTURE NOTES

SESSION TWO: WHY RUN?

The Warm-up

As a new runner, I was impossible to live with at times – ask my husband! I would complain about how difficult and stupid running was as I trailed behind him on our evening runs. I complained *so* much, but I did have a *desire* to learn. My husband would lace up daily and return so refueled and refreshed that I wanted to know about that and experience that. I would say to myself …

"I can't learn how; I don't have time; I am too tired; I am not motivated; it is so hot *outside; it is so* cold *outside; I don't want people to see me because I feel fatter than the other runners; I don't want to do anything too difficult; I do* not *have enough oxygen to get me to the end of the block!"*

All this monkey chatter would rule my world. So I broke away from the chatter and decided to *Run.*

I may run fast or slow, short distances or long, in good weather and bad, and with my dog, husband, friend, or children, or alone. I may run on school tracks, on country roads, up north, down south, on the beach, along a beautiful lake, next to busy streets. Running can be easy one day and grueling the next. I can have great runs that fly by, or short runs that I slog through. I may run in my new pink neon shoes, or in my old garden beater sneakers. Some days I am so excited to hit the pavement running, but *most of the time* I have to haul my lazy, unmotivated self through the front door because, *of course*, I would rather play on my phone, pinning stuff to my Pinterest board, while sipping a great cup of coffee.

I am *not* super-crazy-in-love with running! I wish I did have a stronger attitude! Want running advice? You can find a much wiser guide than me, but *I will not quit* Running and striving to become as strong mentally, physically, and spiritually as God sees fit for my unique Race.

Why run? There are many reasons people run – some personal, some physical, some mental, and some crazy! For me, I keep a convincing list of "why I run" on the front burner of my mind because sometimes I need to remind myself – inspire myself, again – to get out there. Here are a few …

> … I like to push a little further, and I like the "runner's high" that comes with vigorous exercise.
> … I like reaching a goal, such as a race. Accomplishment feels good.
> … The only bad run is the run I do not take!

After running for five years, I tackled my first marathon, the Chicago Marathon, in 2012. Yes!

I finished! I may not have had the best time, even for my age group, but I finished in a fast five hours!

My big, audacious, hairy goal for the next marathon is to shave some hair … oops! … *time* off!

It is amazing how running will force you to go beyond yourself.

The same is true spiritually. The last two years I have been taking notes and studying the analogies between physical running and Spiritually Running. *Wow.* The Lord has taught me so much through the apostle Paul! Paul was the one who first compared the Christian life to running in a race. I started to notice that at points in my spiritual Race, it seemed as if I was Running around and around in the same circle, with no sense of direction. It was repetition and religious routines. I was on a treadmill instead of lifting my head to see real scenery.

Our spiritual Races all have Starting Lines – which was last week's focus –middles, and Finish Lines. Our stories in life are told step by step and mile by mile, and our pace and focus and timing and strategy will help us cross the Finish Line and hear, "Well done." Our physical race is a metaphor for the Christian life because Jesus lived this way! He was always *on the run* to spread the truth about God's goodness and faithfulness and our Finish Line; it is He who throws Himself over the line separating life from death and allows us to finish in victory. I run … and Run my spiritual Race, my friends, because the possibilities for my life extend far beyond the mortal. Let us Run and not be weary, Walk and not faint, in every season of our lives. Let's persevere with purpose. No more Running in circles. Let's Run with His wind at our backs, always and only.

SESSION TWO: WHY RUN?

Day One "Hope Will Chase You Down"

THE COLLISION WITH HOPE:

And hope does not disappoint us, because God has poured out his
love into our hearts by the Holy Spirit, whom he has given us.
Romans 5:5

For in this hope we were saved. But hope that is seen is no
hope at all. Who hopes for what he already has? But if we hope
for what we do not yet have, we wait for it patiently.
Romans 8:24–25

Read all of Acts chapter 26. This is the record of the third, and final, account of Paul's conversion in the Book of Acts. "Conversion" means to change something into a different form, to be used in a different way.

Hope **found Paul.**

Paul the Apostle was one of the most influential early Christian leaders, but before his conversion, he was known for zealously persecuting the newly forming Church and hunting down these believers of Jesus. In verses 12–15 of Acts 26, we see Paul's Race change in a dramatic way. Paul would go on to write almost half of the books in the New Testament, and is considered one of the greatest religious leaders of all Christian history. He spread the Good News across the Roman Empire, including much of Asia, and planted at least three churches in Europe.

In Acts 26, we read about Paul giving his testimony, his unique *story*. Today, I challenge you to use this tool, this outline, of Paul's testimony to formulate your own. As we take our stories apart and look at the pieces, we might see God's hand at work in new ways. It is crucial to be aware of God's preparation in our lives. He stands in our yesterdays, todays, and tomorrows, so God sees all and knows the perfect route to prepare us for every event in our lives.

1. *Hope stopped Saul.* Acts 26:1–15

> This road of Paul's has a sudden turning point. On his approach to Damascus, when he had hoped to put a stop to the spread of "The Way" (a common name for early Christianity) in Jerusalem, God instead stopped him in his tracks with a beam of light that would change his life, and eventually, world history. Isn't it a great feeling to know that God will Run down those dusty, dirty roads after us? However many times we need to be knocked down on our Race to really hear God's voice calling us, He will stay the course with us and be there for the rescue.
>
> Is there a time you can point to in your story when you found yourself knocked down, and asked: "Who are you? What do you want from me?" Describe it below. _____

At this point in Paul's story, he was helpless and broken. Being broken is a great sacrifice before the Lord, and it can be a new Starting Line for us, wherever we are. Paul was still "Saul" at this point, and he was experiencing a godly sorrow for his actions. Saul ached to be restored and at peace with his Father.

Look up Psalm 51:17 and write it below. _____

Circle the word "broken." Take a moment and sow these lines into your heart and consideration before the Lord. Allow God to extend His light and grace – allow a little of His "heatstroke" to restore you.

For some, His light will reveal an area of His prodding and you will have felt that holy goad. For others, it may be a little skip-dance of celebration, remembering His goad, your obedience, and the restoration that followed. Some may need to declare out loud the end of the verse: "O God, you will not despise." Scribble what floats up. And then …

Praise God for this hard work and rock-bottom digging! As with Paul, God will soon pull your hidden strengths into His piercing light and set them (back) onto the right path.

Take a deep breath, as we continue Running …

GOAD

"It is hard for you to kick against the goads."
Acts 26:14b

A "goad" was a stick, nine feet in length and sharpened at one end, for poking at cattle. The cattle could try to kick back, but the length meant the hoof could not reach the herdsman. This passage is generally interpreted as meaning that Paul should not resist the divine force that was moving him in a new direction.

2. *Hope will send you.*

> *Now get up and stand on your feet. I have appeared to you to appoint you as a servant and as a witness of what you have seen of me and what I will show you. I will rescue you from your own people and from the Gentiles. I am sending you to them to open their eyes and turn them from darkness to light, and from the power of Satan to God, so that they may receive forgiveness of sins and a place among those who are sanctified by faith in me. (Acts 26:16–18)*

Don't you love how God calls us out of our failures and sends us immediately in a new direction with a new vision and a new plan?

See, I am doing a new thing! Now it springs up; do you not perceive it? I am making a way in the desert and streams in the wasteland. (Isaiah 43:19)

If you have another Bible available to you (or can find the reference online), take a moment and write out Isaiah 43:19 in another translation. Highlight the areas that stir your spirit. _____

I love the part of the verse that asks us a question: "Do you not perceive it?" Our perspective is the steering wheel of our lives; it influences what we see, as well as how we think, act, and respond to people, places, emotions, situations. If our perspective is faulty, we can run ourselves ragged in all the wrong directions. Paul had to make a choice after he was knocked down, to *sit up* and then *stand up* on his feet in order to *agree* with God's perspective.

Sometimes …
A breakdown with *God needs to happen before*
A breakthrough from *God.*

In what areas will you choose to surrender to God and agree with His perspective? _____

Are you able to perceive a *new direction* God is sending you in? _____

This means that anyone who belongs to Christ has become a new person. The old life is gone and a new life has begun. (2 Corinthians 5:17)

3. *Hope will strengthen you.* (Acts 26:20–22)

I have had God's help to this very day, and so I stand ... (Acts 26:22)

Paul testifies that God's purpose and strength will enable us to move forward despite our struggles and setbacks. It is all about *His Super in our Natural*! (Go ahead and circle it ... it's a great line!)

Paul realized he was going to experience consequences and setbacks due to his former life. However, this time was different because he fully allowed God to lead, guide, and direct his life and new journey.

Let's pause here for a moment. At this point, you may be thinking, "Yeah, been here, done that," or "I have tried, and failed, so many times on this one Race, so ... why bother?" You may love the digging in the Word and the passion of the words and the lure of hope dangled, but may not really believe change in "this" area is truly possible. You'll play along, but you don't really see it. Is this striking a chord?

Sometimes it can feel like we will always be up against mountains. And that one mountain in particular. That may be true, except that each time we allow God to take us through our obstacles without trying to grab the reins back, we get to see Him show off His unlimited power in our lives and circumstances! And when we come out the other side, we realize that those mountains *never* had the power to block our paths, except for the power we handed over to them. This time can be different if we fully allow God to lead, guide, and direct our lives and new journeys.

For the eyes of the Lord run *to and fro throughout the whole earth, to show Himself strong on behalf of those whose heart is loyal to Him. (2 Chronicles 16:9) (NKJV)*

How has God strengthened you and carried you through hard times when you (in the flesh) did not have the strength to go on? _____

In what areas of your life could your load be lifted?

_____

TRAINING TIP: *Remember, you may be in a season in which you really do not feel like moving. Allow God to swoop in like the Hero He is and provide a walker, an elevator, a piggy-back ride, a set of wheels – whatever is needed! – as He embraces, strengthens, and comforts you until your spirit is ready to Run again!*

4. *Hope will stretch you.* (Acts 26:24–29)

We talked some about stretching in last week's "Extra Lap" lesson with tents. Read Acts 26:24–29, and pay particular attention to verse 24. (Yes, read it now.)

Don't you absolutely *love* verse 24? Festus apparently felt that Paul's intense study of the scriptures had led him to a point of mania about resurrection and prophecy. You get the impression that Festus thought it was just fine to study scripture – like a hobby – in one's spare time, perhaps? But to take scripture *so seriously* and *literally*? Why, that's insanity!

Paul responds: "What I am saying is *true* and *reasonable.*"

Paul was being stretched by Truth. God began a new work in Paul and stretched him past his pain and failure – and past his past! God was beginning to stretch him into unknown territory and with new purposes. God was stretching Paul's thinking and understanding.

The same thing will happen to you.

As you begin to handle God's Truth and reason with it, and to let His voice (through the Holy Spirit) turn this over in you and cause new baby green shoots to sprout up, you will be *stretched.* God will stretch the Truth over the hurt areas, and then help you learn and grow and heal and experience Him in new ways – crazy good and wonderful ways!

5. *Hope satisfies you.* (Acts 26:19)

I was not disobedient to the vision from heaven. (Acts 26:19)

Paul uses a double negative here for emphasis. Have you ever tried to bring the full force of your point, or your denial, to something? Your voice might get louder and more emotional, you might gesture with your hands, you might insist that you are not … *not* … *NOT* … responsible! Paul is underscoring here, and it is worth that underscore.

You see, when God gives you a heavenly vision, a calling has been set in motion on your life.

The vision involves a calling. God expects you to respond.

It is in our obedience, our strong and quick obedience, that we find the satisfaction and joy that God wants us to experience. He created us, He knows us – and when we are under the full current of His sweet spot for us?

Yeah. *Sweet.*

A heavenly vision will always begin with a heavenly concern, and when you get the call, you have been enlisted to be a part of God's response to the heavenly concern. In Christ, you will be recruited multiple – hundreds? – of times over the course of your life. The more you respond with obedience, the more you will hear Him, crave His mission, and hunger to be called again.

Has God placed a vision on your heart that He has been stirring around? As you just read the question, something popped up in you.

What was it, in just two words?
_____

Pray through the obedience and the vision.

SESSION TWO: WHY RUN?

Day Two "Get In Shape"

During Paul's time, the Greek athletes displayed tremendous dedication to training for the games we now know as the Olympics. Athletes went to great lengths and abused their bodies to gain competitive advantage. These sacrifices were made so that when the race was won, they could receive a crown made of laurel or olive leaves.

Paul tells us in 1 Corinthians to *run in such a way.* He was encouraging us to get in better spiritual shape in order to succeed. Just as athletes trained with focused and strategic plans for success – trading daily pleasures for exhaustive training – so we are to be self-disciplined into a singleness of purpose.

Much of the text in 1 Corinthians 9 deals with our freedom as Christians. Paul speaks of the law and how he has changed his approach so as to relate more easily to all types of people when spreading the gospel. *Paul's point is that we are free to plan our faith.* Are we disciplined in our walks with Christ? Do we work thoughtfully toward successful outcomes? If an athlete will train extremely hard to win a crown of leaves, how hard should a Christian Train to win the crown of eternal life?

This is our focus today. What shape are you in?

Many believers today would express that they're in good shape, functionally sound, and pretty sturdy. Others may be experiencing *bent* seasons of life. The challenges and issues of life can bend us out of shape: when something or someone important to us gets distorted, misrepresented, falsified, injured, betrayed, disappointed … that can trigger stunted growth or twisting of our growth pattern. Gnarly vines of anger, confusion, hurt, and offense can alter God's best.

So the question: how straight and intentional is your growth pattern?

"Shape" in Greek translates to *morph* (a synonym for "conversion", which we worked with yesterday). You've no doubt heard the term "morph" before! "Morphing" is a special effect in films and animation, and it means that an image changes – or morphs – into another image in a seamless transition. Most often, it is used to depict one person *turning into another.*

So the question: *Who are you turning into?*

> *"Examine yourselves as to whether you are in the faith; test yourselves." 2 Corinthians 13:5*

It is a healthy exercise to regularly examine our patterns, goals, and progress. Are we in alignment with Running in such a way? When we are getting in shape physically, we do things such as standing on scales to weigh ourselves and measuring how long we can go. So how does that translate into spiritual assessment?

We need to weigh ourselves on God's words and His definition of progress and Training and getting in shape. When we consult God through His Word and the Holy Spirit, He can can direct the way we are morphing, how fast we are growing, and what bent parts need to be straightened out. He will gradually change us – if we look to Him ... to take on *His* shape, *His* likeness, *His* perspective, *His* language.

So, ask the questions:

1. Do you feel like you're in pretty good shape, and that you are comfortable with your life and your relationship with God?

2. Has an event in your life caused you to twist out of shape by pushing you into a bent or gnarly posture? Has your growth been stunted or mishapen?

3. Are you trying to get into shape, but finding that the force of the culture's influence … or your work environment … or relational stresses … or your own tiredness or health issues … just make you want to crawl back over to the couch instead?

Look up Job 14:14 and write it below. _____

Job felt that if there was hope of life after death, he could endure his present struggle (depicted in Job 7). Job understood the truth of the resurrection. In the NIV translation, Job refers to waiting for his "renewal" to come. In other translations, you will see the word "change" or "relief" used. The original Hebrew word in this text is used elsewhere in scripture to denote a hoped-for change. In Job's case, the hoped-for change was that of a new life of fellowship and communion with God.

What is your hoped-for change? Go ahead and use the imagination God gave you and project it out in various areas of your life. Describe below the picture or vision that springs to mind. What does it look like … in your friendships? … in your marriage? … in your finances? … in your attitude? _____

In today's and tomorrow's work, we are going to look at some structures to help us assess and examine *in new ways*. If we don't know exactly where we *are*, we cannot effectively come up with plans for faith and what shape we want to *become*.

Today, we're going to sharpen ourselves against one of God's beautiful creations: the butterfly. I love butterflies! I find them to be some of the most remarkable creatures on the planet. They are such beauties, and their life cycle carries a lot of meaning and symbolism that can be useful in evaluating the Christian life.

Many of us have experienced our own "metamorphoses" in becoming new creatures in Christ. But if we look more closely, there is another parallel. This transformation, or metamorphosis, almost never happens at the snap of a finger! We are shaped in stages. Sometimes those stages are painful or uncomfortable, but in the end, the new Life takes flight and *soars*! For each stage of the butterfly's development, there is a brief description. Consider each stage, apply it metaphorically to your Run, and see where God leads you in the process.

Egg stage: The eggs are very small, and laid on a plant. This plant can later be used as food for hatching caterpillars. Eggs are laid in the spring, summer, and fall. Many are laid so that at least some survive.

When we begin to walk with Christ, we start out tiny and fragile. We need to stay with like-minded people to protect our development. Do you relate to this stage?

Larva, the feeding stage (caterpillar): The job of the caterpillar is to eat and eat and eat. As the caterpillar grows, it splits its skin and sheds it four or five times. Food eaten at this time is stored and used at the adult stage. Caterpillars can grow 100 times their size during the larva stage.

This is a growing and expanding stage. As you grow in Christ, your past sometimes does not seem to fit in with your present life. Have you experienced change as you have grown in your cocoon?

Pupa, the transition stage (chrysalis): It may look like nothing is going on, but big changes are happening on the inside. Special cells that were present in the larva are now growing rapidly and will become legs, wings, eyes, antennae, and other parts.

As we go through change, God may require us to become transparent. How have you taken steps to trust and share? _____

Adult, the reproductive stage: In its new adult form, the butterfly emerges, wet and shaky from the cocoon. As blood flows into the wings, the adult flutters them, and when the wings are dry, lifts off … at last. A primary function of the adult stage is to reproduce.

We are all unique, and were created for specific plans designed by God. He puts wings to your story. Has a ministry been birthed in you? A bigger dream? Do you feel called to fly with the Gospel? _____

SESSION TWO: WHY RUN?

Day Three "The Stages of a Runner"

My first few runs happened back in 2006. I was excited to feel like I had accomplished something! But man, I was so sore after those first few runs – and my knees swelled up like basketballs, which, of course, made them so very attractive on my already stocky legs!

Progress is a matter of learning, maturing, and developing tenacity through hardship and obstacles. Swollen knees from a first run ... the wobbly knees of tepid faith ... the calloused "knees" of a prayer warrior ... We can draw parallel after parallel between the physical runner and the God-seeking Runner. That's exactly what Paul did in so many of his New Testament letters. So let's play Paul today! We are going to examine the stages of a physical runner while walking right alongside Elijah and Elisha as we pose the question: how far do *you* want to go? Picture a voice in your ear: "You've got this ... *Run!*"

Read 2 Kings 2:1–10.

Elisha went from being a plowman working in the fields one day, to a prophet of the Lord the next. In this incident, Elijah repeatedly urged Elisha to remain behind, perhaps to test his determination to be formally recognized as Elijah's successor. Persistence is a key trait of faithful prophets. We will examine the four places mentioned in 2 Kings (Gilgal, Bethel, Jericho, and the Jordan), as they are highly significant in Israel's history and symbolic of stages in the Christian's life.

STAGE 1 Runner: beginner
STAGE 1 Christ-follower: Gilgal, the place of separation.

The early stages are precarious for a beginning runner. The runner is perched on the edge of something brand new, and the old self, the old habits and patterns, and outside opinions from others will rise up and bark ferociously. There is an energy burst with the "newness," but once that wears off, it can be difficult to head out for the daily run.

The first stop in this Run is Gilgal, a place of great significance in Israel's history. In Joshua 2, this account is told of the Israelites: They had departed from Egypt and wandered for 40 years in the desert. In that time, the original Israelite men coming out of Egypt had died off, and none of those born since had been circumcised. (Circumcision was a sign of the covenant between a man and God, ordered by God and begun with Abraham.) The practice had stopped in the wandering 40 years because the Israelites had been unbelieving and disobedient during that time. In the Joshua account, God revived this act of covenant so that Israel would once again become children of Abraham and heirs of the Promised Land. Verse 9 recounts that at this point, the Lord declared to Joshua, "Today I have rolled away the reproach of Egypt from you." The place was called Gilgal, which literally means "rolling" or "rolled away," and symbolically stands for *separation* – being separated from the past and separated unto God.

This is where Elisha started, and spiritually it is where we all start. We should be separated from all that would seek to draw us away from God, and set apart – *to* God – as living sacrifices. God called Israel to a place where they saw themselves as they were *in Him*: obedient, trusting, faithful.

Look up Colossians 3:3 and write it below. _____

Do you see it? This is the same work God wants to do in us! Allow Him to cut away all that He does not want in your life; let Him circumcise that which should not be there. Let Him roll away the reproach of bitterness, failure, poverty, unforgiveness, defeat, hurt, and shame. *Reclaim* that which is your inheritance, your Promised Land, in Christ.

What is your personal Gilgal? Can you pinpoint a place of separating that God is doing in you?

_____

STAGE 2 Runner: jogger
STAGE 2 Christ-follower: Bethel, the house of God.

The jogger is now feeling secure in the run. The jogger might still be intimidated by the high achieving of competitors and marathoners, but the jogger has made a significant break from the couch-potato days. The runs are satisfying, there is a glow after the run, and the jogger will eagerly resume running after injury or foul weather because the habit/practice now defines them.

> *Elijah said to Elisha, "Stay here; the LORD has sent me to Bethel." But Elisha said, "As surely as the LORD lives and as you live, I will not leave you." So they went down to Bethel. (2 Kings 2:2)*

Elisha is persistent and tenacious with Elijah, and they journey on to Bethel. We first hear of Bethel in Genesis 28:10–19. Read the passage. (This is an important connection.)

So Bethel was named by Jacob, literally "House of God," because Jacob had had this *amazing* time with God; he had been in the presence of the *Lord*! Bethel speaks to us about the Lord's presence – and our growing hunger to *be there*. And yet, it can be here on the Jogger path that the lure of the world raises its ugly head. What we have clearly been *separated* from can come crawling back to entice us. Bethel reminds us of how sweet it is to find ourselves in the House of God; how amazing it is to live our lives filled with peace and hope. The world does not know peace like we do. Like Elisha, we are to persist and pursue, and not fall back onto the couch. We have a mantel to claim; it is worth the journey.

Pursue that Runner's high. What is your personal Bethel? Can you pinpoint some habits or practices in your Bethel?

STAGE 3 Runner: competitor
STAGE 3 Christ-follower: Jericho, Walk by faith.

The competitive streak reveals itself after awhile. Although the competitive urge can be a great motivator, stimulating the runner to train well and push through obstacles, the urge can also rear an ugly head: the "win" is no longer achieving one's personal best, but comparing oneself to others.

The next stop for Elisha and Elijah was Jericho. The story is told in Joshua chapter 6:1–27. This is a familiar story. (If it isn't, please read the account in Joshua 6.) The Israelites encounter a decisive battle in Jericho, and need to win the battle in order to establish a path to the new homeland. Jericho was a walled city and presented a major obstacle. The King of Jericho denied the Israelites passage through, so they were stuck with three options:

1. Defeat Jericho and pass into the Promised Land.
2. Join Jericho and be assimilated into its culture and belief system.
3. Stay out in the wilderness and die.

The Lord told Joshua they were going to go with plan #1 and that He, the Lord, had already delivered Jericho into the Israelites' hands. They simply had to go with God's way of doing things. They were to march around the city walls for six days with the ark, with priests blowing rams' horns in declaration. On the seventh day, the priests were to give a long blast on the horns, and all the Israelites were, at that point, to give a loud shout, and the walls would tumble down.

Let's pause for a moment to see what this story can mean in our context. We've got history's first speed-marchers circling Jericho, a walled and fortified city. Just imagine how the residents of Jericho were reacting. Do you suppose they were jeering and hooting? Laughing? Mocking? Wouldn't God's way of doing things have mystified them?

What about your Jericho? Our Jericho-obstacles are there because Satan knows that a frustrated Christian is an ineffective Christian. Our enemy knows that the Christian who is dancing in the House of God and swimming in the blessing of Christ is Running a great Race! And a confident Runner is spreading the Kingdom of God to the far reaches of the earth. Therefore, Satan will do anything in his power to keep us feeling defeated and scared – he wants us to *quit*.

What is your Jericho?

Look up Psalm 18:29 and write it below.

_____

STAGE 4 Runner: athlete
STAGE 4 Christ-follower: Jordan

The athlete stage is when the runner finds more meaning in the drive to fulfill their potential than in compulsively collecting times and trophies. Being an athlete is a state of mind that is not bound by age, performance, or place in the pack. The *competitor* stage ties victory and defeat solely to performance. The *athlete* stage means that victory is in the quality of effort.

The final test for Elisha came with the Jordan.

The Israelites crossed over the Jordan waters to get into the Promised Land. God had miraculously separated the waters for the Israelites to pass (similar to God's pushing back the wall of water of the Red Sea for them to leave Egypt), and so the Jordan was a highly significant place in Israelite history. The miracle testified through the land, and through the generations, of the might of God.

The Jordan is a place of transformation, and a dividing line. It was here – long after the time of Joshua – that Elisha picked up the mantel from Elijah after Elijah was gathered up into the heavens. God chose Elisha. Elisha persevered during testing. Elisha picked up the mantel.

So what mantel are you to pick up? What are you to take on? Describe where you think God may be leading you.

Critical question: Did *God* part the waters for you? Or did you get in there with a bucket and determine that you were going to bail yourself into this dream?

Here's the thing. *There may come a time when we get so caught up in our visions for ourselves that we fade away from Running with Jesus. We can become unbalanced Runners when our stories claim more value in our hearts than God's story for the world. Pace your breathing by returning to the Breath of Heaven. The Holy Spirit can rein in any flailing arms and mis-timed steps and get you back on course. We will pick up this theme in tomorrow's work.*

SESSION TWO: WHY RUN?

Day Four "It's all About the Glory"

Am I now trying to win the approval of people, or God?
Or am I striving to please people? If I were still trying to
please people, I would not be a slave of Christ."
(Galatians 1:10, HCSB)

I am an ordinary gal and a rookie physical runner. I try to live a life aimed after the glory of God. My spiritual Race began 16 years ago and I desire to Run for His glory, because when I crossed the line of faith I realized that my Race – my life – was for my Savior God. God is the one who gives me strength and helps me Run. I wouldn't get very far, and certainly wouldn't be able to finish well, if it weren't for Him. I can easily get distracted and sidetracked, and sometimes I slow down, but I know that God will take care of me along the journey and reconfigure my track lanes throughout the day!

It is God who arms me with strength and makes my way perfect. He makes my
feet like the feet of a deer; he enables me to stand on the heights … You broaden
the path beneath me so that my ankles do not turn. Psalm 18: 32–33, 36.

Before we go one sentence further, please pause and pray, asking God to be with you every step of the way. God desires to show you His glory, so let's ask Him for it.

Prayer: Father God, help me *Run* into Your glory so that I may have the heartbeat of Your presence *within* all the running around I will do today and in the days ahead. I commit to learning how to be completely dependent on You, and to look for Your glory throughout my days.

We learned in Day Three that God often molds us in stages, that growth is layered upon the victories we achieve, and that we need to be confident that we are seeking God's glory in our Races, not our own. The glory of God is our focus today.

> *"And all of us, as with unveiled face, [because we] continued to behold [in the Word of God] as in a mirror the glory of the Lord, are constantly being transfigured into His very own image in ever-increasing splendor and from one degree of glory to another; for this comes from the Lord, [who is] the Spirit." 2 Corinthians 3:18 (Amplified)*

The Lord greatly desires for us to Run in such a way that He can show off His glory in our everyday Races!

God promises His presence to Moses in Exodus 33. Let's learn to apply this truth and Run in a way that we get to experience the *glory* of an amazing God!

Read the passage below from Exodus 33: 12–19.

> *Moses said to the Lord, "You have been telling me, 'Lead these people,' but you have not let me know whom you will send with me. You have said, 'I know you by name and you have found favor with me.' If you are pleased with me, teach me your ways so I may know you and continue to find favor with you. Remember that this nation is your people."*
>
> *The Lord replied, "My Presence will go with you, and I will give you rest."*
>
> *Then Moses said to him, "If your presence does not go with us, do not send us up from here. How will anyone know that you are pleased with me and with your people unless you go with us? What else will distinguish me and your people from all the other people on the face of the earth?"*
>
> *And the Lord said to Moses, "I will do the very thing you have asked, because I am pleased with you and I know you by name."*
>
> *Then Moses said, "Now show me your glory."*
>
> *And the Lord said, "I will cause all my goodness to pass in front of you, and I will proclaim my name, the Lord, in your presence. I will have mercy on whom I will have mercy, and I will have compassion on whom I will have compassion."*

Look up Psalm 25:4–5 and write it below. _____

_____

Now go back up to the verse you just wrote, and circle all the action words in this verse. *Use this verse and pray through it daily over your life. It will have you Running into the Glory of God in no time!*

Christ desires to work in us to bring us to His glorious image and His plans for our lives, but how does this really happen? Moses wanted to *see the glory of God* in his present situation.

Do you want to *see the glory of God* in your present situation?

Let's dip back into the Exodus account of Moses' interaction with the Lord, and see what we can glean from it.

TRAINING TIP #1: We miss seeing the Glory pass by because we simply do not ask to see it! In verse 18, Moses *asks*: "Now show me your glory."

Look up Proverbs 13:12 and write it below. _____

_____

There is an interesting word tucked in there: *deferred*, specifically *hope deferred*. You know what this is. We all have that resolution to an issue that is not-yet.

We have the setback that comes with the start-all-over-again. And again.

We have the longing in our hearts for something that seems so far off.

We can't see beyond the stress of today, but we know Hope is in there somewhere.

Ask God to see His Glory in your deferred situation.

Take a moment and write out a few places where you would like to see the Glory of God pass by …

… now take a moment and give them to God.

TRAINING TIP #2: We miss the Glory of God because we are not in a place to receive it or notice it pass by.

Later, in Exodus 33:21, God instructs Moses *where* to stand. "There is a place near me where you may stand …" and in 34:2, God instructs Moses *when* to stand. After Moses is given instructions to carve out what we know as the Ten Commandments, the Lord says, "Be ready in the morning …"

To see His Glory, we have to be positioned *so that we are ready and He alone is in our line of sight.*

Ask yourself:

How is my attitude in my current situation?

How am I making the time to present myself to God daily, like Moses did?

Am I alert to Satan's lies about myself or my situation? Lies that could distort my vision?

The God of the mountaintop who speaks to us from the clouds and causes His glory to pass before us *is the same God* who will appear to us in the valleys. Don't fall and forget to get up! Go to your secret place, the cleft of the Rock, and let God tend to you in prayer. Then ask Him again for a peek at His glory in your life, and be encouraged. Don't trust your feelings; trust what, and *whom*, you *know*.

TRAINING TIP #3: We need to expect the Glory to show up in unique forms.

We need to remember that God is in the good times, and He is fully in our hard times also. That can be hard to remember when our attitudes, emotions, and fears blind us to seeing His Glory.

The problem … gives us fresh direction >>>>>>>> to push us into His Glory

The problem … tests us >>>>>>>> pushing us into His Glory

The problem … helps us grow >>>>>>>> by pushing us into His Glory

Take a minute to write down when you have seen the Glory of God (His radiance, His God-ness, His divine activity, His Show) in your life, and how He came through with fresh direction or protection, or answers "dropped into your head," or He grew you into a stronger *Runner.*

God uses everything in our lives so that we can be a window "showcase" of His Glory.

If you were a window showcase and people were in town, shopping and strolling by and looking in at all the displays in the store windows … would those shoppers passing by be able to see Jesus in your life? What in your showcase would make people stop at your window? And in those things that caught their attention, how would they see God's glory? Looking at your "showcase window," would they feel compelled to come in?

Jot down some notes and be ready to share your "showcase vision" with your group this week.

Mile Marker

Jodi

Sometimes the most difficult thing for a person
of faith to see is the big picture.
God and I both knew I was finally ripe and ready − I was tired
of being spiritually stagnant, with no direction or purpose. For
two years I patiently prayed for God to lead me to "the place"
where I was ready to grow next. I was empty, ready to be filled.
Well, I can say, our God, in His all-knowing infinite wisdom,
decided to fulfill *more* than what I thought I needed.
One unsuspecting evening, I was leaving church out of an entrance I
never park at, but did that day. I was almost out the door when I was
stopped by someone who excitedly asked if I was joining the Marathon
team, because "all the people from our old small group are running it,"
she said. (Peer pressure is real, folks!) It seems so ridiculous to me now,
but as I was deriving excuses for saying "no," all that was coming out
of me was my fears about fundraising − nevermind the 26.2 miles.
Truthfully, I didn't need to pray about it − I knew this was
too wild to not be *it*. That's just like God, to lay a challenge
before you that you never dreamed you would ever do − and
it wasn't anywhere near my bucket list, I assure you.

The next thing I knew, God moved my 42-year-old, *never-broke-
an-athletic-sweat-in-my-life* body and had me train for eight months
to run the 2012 *Chicago Marathon* for the World Vision charity.
I went on and ran the Detroit half-marathon the next year.

All of this blew me away, as I would never have guessed that running would transform my life as it has in so many ways.

God still continues to amaze me. (I hope that never
changes; I like being amazed – it makes me smile.)
It was truly a blessing to have a *Purpose* to all this running that I would
be doing. God fulfilled my need to serve Him differently by allowing
me to run for his children in Africa, who desperately needed clean
water. Those beautiful people I ran for turned out to be a huge blessing
for my life. God's timing is perfect. I honestly didn't know if I could
do it, but I had peace about me because I believed God would not lay
this opportunity out for me if He didn't think I could do it. In my mind
I aligned this goal God had set before me as an outward challenge
to prove to myself that I had what it took to sacrifice for *Him*.

Looking back, God's plan was perfect. I finally started
something and *finished it!* I ran 26.2 miles! But that
actually is just the beginning of a new chapter …

Along the path I lost weight, got healthy, increased my spiritual
growth, rid myself of the mask that prevented genuine joy, learned
to live outside the box, became more transparent, increased my
confidence, and placed countless wonderful people in my life and
gained some amazing new friends to share life with. I am also
now a running lifer. It is empowering and life changing to know
you can accomplish anything with perseverance and God.

*"And not only that, but we also boast in our sufferings, knowing that suffering
produces endurance, and endurance produces character, and character produces
hope, and hope does not disappoint us, because God's love has been poured
into our hearts through the Holy Spirit that has been given to us."*
Romans 5:3–5

SESSION TWO: WHY RUN?

Day Five Personal Running Log

Pace yourself

Review the week's work: the scripture you have covered, the writings on the lines and in the margins. What would you ask God for this day? What did you not quite get this week? How can you serve Him more? Who and what should you be praying for?

P Pray.
A Ask for God's vision for your life.
C Communicate back to God.
E Enter His Race for your life.

Run free in the space below: _____

Recovery questions

***What main thing did the study push me to *do, be,* or *feel* as a result of the material?

***What did God say to me through this week?

***How is my Run measuring up to this word? What action(s) will I take to bring my life in line with the word/message received this week?

My challenge

With what truth do I need to study and Train harder?

BLISTER:

"Ouch and Pinch": Jot down those moments this week that caused pain.

BLISS:

"Praise You and Thank You": Jot down your praises.

Team Spirit/Sharing Challenge: Think of someone you know who is limping right now. _____

Pray for them.

Look for an opportunity to share with them what you have learned this week.

Theme verse:

Do you not know that in a race all the runners run, but only one gets the prize? Run in such a way as to get the prize. Everyone who competes in the games goes into strict training. They do it to get a crown that will not last; but we do it to get a crown that will last forever. Therefore, I do not run like a man running aimlessly; I do not fight like a man beating the air. No, I beat my body and make it my slave so that after I have preached to others, I myself will not be disqualified for the prize. (1 Corinthians 9: 24–27)

Write out the verses in the space below.

Pray the verses back to God, making them personal.

When you've memorized them, share *the verses by speaking them out loud to your small group!* Great job!

The Extra Lap

Earlier this week, we looked at how Hope completely upended Paul's life, focus, and future. When God steps in, all bets are off!

You were encouraged to chart out your own story under the headlines of "Hope …" What follows is a brief glimpse into my story, outlined by Hope.

We begin with some background …

"I did not much value who I was or what I had to offer, so I consistently sold myself short and made many bad choices throughout high school and college. I was never told that God had big plans for me … instead, I knew that the devil couldn't tell me anything about myself that I didn't already believe. I developed earlier than other girls, and had bushy eyebrows and a five o'clock shadow on my chin! I was a cute girl – but those things bothered the absolute mess out of me. I was athletic (figure skating) until I dropped out because I thought everyone else was better than me. I was a cheerleader, but the biggest girl on the squad. I will never forget being told by a boy that I had tree-trunk legs. My Jordache jeans (remember those?) never fit like everyone else's, and I hated shopping for swimsuits I could stuff my breasts into. You'd never know I was miserable, though. On the outside, I was the popular, happy, smart girl with great stories.

"Fast-forward to college … I drank a lot. I fell out of the back of a pick-up truck when the tailgate dropped open, and my "friends" left me in the road and took off. The injuries were major, and I headed home to heal. Home was not happy – my parents were divorcing after 27 years of marriage. Although they were great

parents, I had no memories of them ever being tender to one another. I craved affection and acceptance. I looked for love in every wrong place. What I would agree to for five minutes of being held afterward! In those five minutes I would pretend that the guy was a real boyfriend and wanted me, and that something in me was lovable. I was used. Rejected. Disillusioned. Desperate.

And now I was pregnant.

"I went to an abortion clinic with a friend, and they said the magic words: "We can take care of this problem quickly, and you'll never think about it again." So I had the abortion, and a cold heart. I felt nothing at that time. I met another man who I thought might actually like me. Did we have a connection? Not really, but it felt good to have someone. And then I found myself pregnant again. And handled it the same way, but this time, guilt *defined me: I was hopeless, consumed with failure and felt frozen in place. Somewhere in me was a good girl who was worthy of a good life, but I had no map to find her. I was separated from God, yet longing for Him. Although I couldn't see it at the time, God started to lead this bent and broken girl back in steps.*

"I met Dan, who is now my husband. He cared for me in a special way, and I could just tell this was different. For one, he had a praying mommy, my friends! Oh, the power of those praying moms! *We married, we struggled, but I was lurching toward the Savior through Dan's family! But then, all the baggage that we both brought into the marriage started to get unpacked, and by our second year of marriage, and my husband's affair, we were broken. It was here, when I wanted to run away from everything –* it was here that I personally collided with Hope Incarnate. ***T****hrough the ministry of a good pastor and the ongoing wisdom and counsel of my mother-in-law, Dan and I learned to allow God to heal us individually and personally through relationships with the Healer and Restorer Himself.*

You see, it is impossible to truly love another person when you desperately despise your messy self. But when two whole and healed people come together? Ah, yes. Now *we were ready for our marriage. Today, I am continuing to fall in love with my husband, and together we are building a marriage of compassion and encouragement and cheering each other on in our Race!*

So, here is my story, charted in Hope:

1. **Hope stopped me.**

After years of brokenness and despair, I was stopped when the marriage crisis hit. *Hope* stopped me in my tracks, and my eyes began to open up to the things of God for the first time. I crossed over the line of faith by putting my hope in Jesus Christ for the first time.

> *Hope deferred makes the heart sick, but the desire brings forth a tree of life.*
> *Proverbs 13:12*

2. **Hope sent me**.

I could not see what was in the distance, but I knew God was working upstream, and for the first time I had peace being in His current.

> Hope encouraged me to rise and stand.
> Hope sent me in a *new* direction.
> Hope was beginning to heal and teach me.

> *Fear not, for you* will not be put to shame; and do not feel humiliated, *for you will not be disgraced; but you will forget the shame of your youth ... For the Lord has called you, like a wife forsaken and grieved in spirit ... (Isaiah 61:7)*

> *Instead of your shame, you shall have double honor, and instead of confusion, they shall rejoice in their portion ... Everlasting joy shall be theirs. (Isaiah 54:4–8, NKJ)*

3. **Hope strengthened me.**

God has helped me to this very day, and so I stand.

I have learned to *Run in such a way*. God's *super* has been poured into my natural, and I have known the power of my Savior encouraging me daily to Run my Race with focus and determination.

4. **Hope stretched me.**

I was no longer able to bury emotions or pretend to "play" life and fake it. During this time in my life, I was ravenous for the Word and for fellowship within the Body of Christ. Friends and family knew of my love of the Word, and began to see me Run in a new way. I began to stretch the truth of God's Word over the issues in my life, and to learn and wrestle and reason with the Word of God. I went through a lot of healing of the deep wounds of my youth and poor choices, and embraced God's forgiveness.

It was an amazing season – some tough training runs – but the stretching strengthened me in the end!

> *Keep guard over your heart, for out of the heart spring the issues in life. (Proverbs 4:23)*

5. **Hope satisfied me.**

For the first time in my life, I am content in my relationships. I have confidence in myself through the grace of God. I have a sense of purpose and destiny, and am motivated to explore and dream big in what God is calling me to do.

My heavenly vision was a component of healing. God led me to understand my gifts and the way He has created me. This kind of intimate knowledge from the Creator is so satisfying. He has emboldened me to share my story and my love for the Word with other hurting people. I can now talk about my abortion experiences and my past hurts without shame, and instead, declare the forgiveness and love of the Savior!

Run in such a way, friends! Run!

Now it's your turn …

Take the five points and chart it out for yourself. It's your story …
Go for it!

1. *Hope stopped me …*

2. *Hope sent me …*

3. *Hope strengthened me …*

4. *Hope stretched me …*

5. *Hope satisfied me …*

SESSION THREE

Run with Tenacity

1 CORINTHIANS 9: 24–27

Do you not know that in a race all the runners run, but only one gets the prize? Run in such a way as to get the prize. Everyone who competes in the games goes into strict training. They do it to get a crown that will not last; but we do it to get a crown that will last forever. Therefore, I do not run like a man running aimlessly; I do not fight like a man beating the air. No, I beat my body and make it my slave so that after I have preached to others, I myself will not be disqualified for the prize.

SESSION THREE: LECTURE NOTES

SESSION THREE: RUN WITH TENACITY

The Warm-up

When you are taking aim at a goal that is very challenging, tenacity is a crucial skill to have in your quiver.

Of course, anything worth doing takes persistence, perseverance, and sometimes a small dose of determined stubbornness! Tenacity is the refined, professional, grown-up, gritted-teeth cousin of stubbornness. It is the groomed and mature version. It fits the Runner well.

Tenacity: "determination, purpose; the quality of being determined to do or achieve something; firmness or purpose."

Runners are tough! They simply don't give up, ever! Write this statement out on the lines provided, and then highlight it to within an inch of its life … or until the ink bleeds through the page! This needs to be internalized.

Every runner learns to handle pain and fatigue on a regular basis because there is no other way to get to the finish line. Runners understand the value of hard work, commitment, and consistency better than anyone else. To persevere, with eyes fixed on the Prize, means dealing with the pain and the trial and the setback with tenacity.

Another word in the "tenacity" family is *resilience*. Resilience is rooted in tenacity of spirit —determination to embrace all that makes life worth living, even in the face of overwhelming odds. And at the core, both words are dependent on a clear sense of identity and purpose: *we are more resilient, more tenacious, because we can hold fast to our vision of a different and better future.*

In watching dedicated runners or other kinds of committed athletes at their "finish lines," we are always impressed by their endurance. Successfully getting to the end is a big accomplishment. However, what comes before the endurance, and what makes the endurance even possible, is all the thousands of tenacity steps that happen along the way. And every single tenacity step involves looking up and seeing the prize and remembering the goal.

God does this in us, as Runners. He pushes us to the next stage of experience and lessons to make us better, stronger, more enduring, more resilient … from one expression of His glory to the next. This is spiritual tenacity, and it's what we're opening up this week.

Let's lace up those Running shoes, Friends, and Run *in such a way!*

SESSION THREE: RUN WITH TENACITY

Day One "Tapping into the Supernatural"

Behold, I will do a marvelous work among this
people, a marvelous work and a wonder.
Isaiah 29:14 (KJV)

In Isaiah chapter 29, God is taking Jerusalem to task for their disobedience and pride, their blindness and their empty, ritualistic worship. It is known as a "woe oracle," meaning that it is rife with judgment and prophetic destruction. The Lord is declaring who He is (sovereign, almighty, powerful) to the foolish arrogance of humankind. The chapter speaks of God's entreaties to man, but man is too dull to comprehend and unwilling to bow. So God makes Himself known again to them – and they still don't get it. And He shows Himself again, and they reject Him. Back and forth goes the chapter, eventually leading to restoration and hope – praise God – and tucked into the middle is *this little line depicting exactly what God can do.* In trying to reach His beloved people, God can *explode* with energy and works and revelations and presence that can Blow. Our. Minds.

The multiple translations throw superlative after superlative at this passage …

SPECTACULAR!
SHOCK.
AMAZE!
ASTOUND.
Miraculous!
CONFOUND.

STARTLE THEM WITH ONE UNEXPECTED BLOW AFTER ANOTHER

We are meant to behold His marvelous works and His wonders.
We are designed to be wonder-filled …
<u>Wonder-full!</u>

(Does that describe your life?)

When I think of my favorite childhood superhero, *I immediately land on Wonder Woman. I remember coming home from school, and the Wonder Woman television show would be on at 4:00 p.m. Wonder Woman was gifted with a wide range of superhuman powers and superior combat and battle skills. She also possessed an arsenal of weapons, including the "Lasso of Truth," a pair of indestructible bracelets, a tiara (which doubled as a projectile), and a beautiful cape. And when the mortal "Diana Prince" needed to transform into Wonder Woman, she would spin and spin. And so would I! I would spin in my bedroom right along with her, and my imagination would take me on capers and justice missions, and I believed and believed …*

> *The trouble was this: on television Diana changed into Wonder Woman.*
> *… in my bedroom, I stayed the same.*

What if we don't have to remain mere mortals?
What if there really are supernatural powers we have access to?

Surely you heard of him and were taught in him in accordance with the truth that is in Jesus. You were taught, with regard to your former way of life, to put off your old self, which is being corrupted by its deceitful desires, to be made new in the attitude of your minds; and to put on the new self, created to be like God in true righteousness and holiness. Ephesians 4:21–24

When we "spin," or, in other words, transform, *our minds into the powerful truth of who God is, we choose to* put on *the supernatural and really see ourselves as who we are in Christ.*

Understanding your identity in Christ is essential to your success at living a victorious life. Let's start with a promise:

Rewrite today's theme verse (at the top of today's homework) below. (Isaiah 29:14)

Because of this I will do wonders among these hypocrites I will show that human wisdom is foolish and even the most brilliant people lack understanding. NKJV- Therefore behold I will again do a marvelous work amongst N this people. A marvelous work and a wonder.

Now, look up Psalm 139:14 and write it below.

NLV Thank you for making me so wonderfully complex your workmenship is marvelous and how well I know it

Compare the two verses. In your own words, what is God saying to you through these verses?

_____

Now, let's get specific about who you are in Christ. Under each headlined description, look up each Bible verse listed and answer the question: "How?" (The first one is done for you as an example.)

1. *I am accepted.*

   John 1:12 (how?) Because I received Jesus, I have the right to become a child of God.

   John 15:15

   Ephesians 1:7

   Ephesians 1:11

2. *I am forgiven.*

   Isaiah 40:2

   Isaiah 61:7

   Isaiah 43:18

3. *I am strengthened.*

   Isaiah 40:29 states: He gives power to the weak, and to those who have no might, he increases strength! So when we spin into His presence by taking the time to learn how to Run in such a way, the power of God:

1 Thessalonians 2:13 *refuels your mind* … How?

Hebrews 12:11–13 *renews your strength* … How?

Romans 12:2 *re-prioritizes your thinking* … How?

4. *I am significant.*

   John 15:16

   Isaiah 42:1

5. *I am a warrior.*

   Psalm 18:29

Why is it important for us to know *who we are in Christ?*

Look up Ephesians 6:12 and write it below. _____

If you used the NIV translation, you opened with the word "struggle." Others use "fight." But the predominant translation describing the battle is *wrestle* (King James, New King James, English Standard, American Standard). We *wrestle.* We do hand-to-hand combat. We take down with force.

This word "wrestle" describes a very popular sport of the ancient Greeks. It was a contest in which one contestant attempted to force his opponent out of a circle, or force him to the ground. It was very physical, and required discipline, training, resolve, and *tenacity.* The Greeks trained boys from a young age, and preparation was considered lifelong.

So our Training is to be lifelong. Believers Train by obeying the discipleship described by Jesus, and through the "crucifying of the flesh" as described by

Paul. We are not to be conformed to the pattern of this world, because God is qualifying and Training us to take the Fight *to* the world as His warriors. The world needs warriors to hold the line and push back the darkness on every level. His supernatural power will be manifested differently in each of us, as He will draw our unique circles out for us and say to us:

"Here is your post. Hold the line. Take it on."

Jesus is the supernatural strength that wonder-filled women have!

Friends, God did not create you to live the spiritual life and Run the Race on your own physical strength. As a matter of fact, as much as I enjoy running, I look forward to my walk breaks when the fatigue sets in. In the Christian Race, we must also have walk breaks to regain focus and keep a good pace.

Paul wrote in Galatians 5:25, "Since we live (Run) by the Spirit, let us keep in step with the Spirit."

When we try to Run on our own power, we become burned out and fatigued, as opposed to a life of peace and a steady pace. My challenge to you: make your body line up, daily, with the Word of God, and accept the Holy Spirit's help to do it. Then you will be victorious in your Run.

Five steps to be wonder-filled and to hold the line like a warrior!

1. Run to God first so you can walk in the Spirit. (Psalm 16:4, Galatians 5:25)
2. Live an exchanged life. (Galatians 2:20)
3. Take off the old and put on the new. (2 Corinthians 5:17)
4. Deny the flesh. (Luke 9:23)
5. Keep the body under control. (1 Corinthians 9:27)

My prayer for you is that when it's time to walk, you will walk out the fear, the struggle, the cramp, the fracture, the disappointment. God will refocus you and bring you up to pace. This is not always an easy Race, but by the power of the Holy Spirit working in you, you can win!

I get so excited – it's my passion to Train others to Run effectively. I am thrilled for you. I believe if God brought you to this page of the study, He is faithful and just, and He does have a plan to guide you through. Jesus is there, my friend. Keep Walking/Running in God's grace.

SESSION THREE: RUN WITH TENACITY

Day Two "Tenacity Calls for Commitment"

Toughness is in the soul and the spirit, not in the muscles.

Commitment determines our direction in life, both in the secular world and in the spiritual realm, so as Christians, we need to possess a *holy determination* to serve, please, and obey God.

Daniel was a man committed to obedience during his times of severe testing. As a result, Daniel's choices were based on his determination to obey, rather than on his life circumstances. Daniel's obedience was pivotal not only to the outcome of his life, but also to the furthering of God's plan in the world. Can God work around our disobedient obstinacy? Of course! In so doing, are we forfeiting something amazing in our lives? Yes. That's where we're landing today.

I don't know about you, but this is a place I get stuck in when I'm Training: I have these great desires to see God do great things through me, but then I also have these days when my commitment and obedience just *fail*! You too?

1. *Daniel stays devoted.*

We are going to hop around the book of Daniel in today's lesson, but let's begin in the first chapter and establish our bearings a little. Some background: the historical setting for this book is during the Babylonian captivity (605 B.C.) King Nebuchadnezzar would lay siege to Judah three times. (The Lord allowed this; see Daniel 1:2.) The book of Daniel opens after the first siege, when Nebuchadnezzar brought Daniel and his friends, along with other captives of the Judean nobility, to Babylon.

This was the Israelite elite class, and these boys (likely around 15 years old) were deemed exceptional (v.4), and to be trained to serve this foreign king. Indoctrination was the goal.

Look up Daniel 1:8 and write it below. _____

Now go back up and circle the word "resolved" in Daniel 1:8. (Some translations may say "purposed in his heart," "set upon his heart," or "determined.") This is *how* Daniel did it: he decided ahead of time and stuck to it. He resolved/purposed/determined that he would obey. And he did.

(Can we give a shout-out to any mothers of 15-year-old sons? Or anyone who has ever known a 15-year-old boy? Is Daniel not *remarkable?*)

Look up James 1:25 and compare it to Daniel 1:8. What does God promise those who determine to obey and *do it?*

What was Daniel standing in obedience to, and why? _____

What delicacies of this world get in your face and try to corrupt you, pulling you away from God's ways and favor? _____

2. *When faced with adversity, Daniel commits to prayer.*

In Daniel 6, Daniel's enemies were setting a trap for him with an edict that anyone who prayed to someone other than the Babylonian king would be thrown into the lion's den. You see, they knew Daniel and were jealous of his influence, but couldn't find any evidence to get rid of him. To get to him, they knew they'd have to go after his Faith-Walk. And they knew to zero in on *prayer*.

How strongly do you radiate that you are a follower of Jesus Christ? Is your faith so radiant and evident that even enemies would notice?

What happened next? **Read Daniel 6:10.**

When he got news of the edict, Daniel's *first* instinct was to pray.

In prayer, he got down on his knees and *gave thanks*.

The last few words of the verse tell us volumes about Daniel: "Just as he had done before."

Prayer was his *habit*, the *rhythm* of his life.

Get ready for something really interesting. (Well, I think so!) Do you remember that in this passage Daniel's enemies were setting a trap for him? Of course you do. Here it comes …

In Aramaic, the word for "prayer" ("slotha") means "to set a trap."

Now don't get your knickers in a knot … let's work this out. "Trap" is a crude translation that, to us, has quite a negative connotation. Turn it a little bit the other way: have you ever noticed that when you pray, "coincidences" start to happen? It is as though in prayer, by speaking the words to the Father, we *set the stage,* in our hearts and minds, for His entrance. It is here that "ideas" and prompting and dreams just drop into our awareness. Or, later in the day something happens, or we "notice" something and think, "Huh. Didn't I just pray that this morning?"

If we don't pray, the curtain will sometimes just stay down, stuck. Prayer creates divine opportunities.

Daniel *made* it his habit, his pattern, his rhythm of opening himself for the divine Entrance.

3. *Daniel displays commitment despite the circumstances.*

We're in the lions' den now. Look up Daniel 6:23 and write it below. _____

Lions were in the den with Daniel. What's prowling around in your den? (Fears, temptations, setbacks?) _____

The last few words of Daniel 6:23 explain how Daniel came out of the den unscathed: *Daniel had* trusted *in his God.*

Look up Daniel 2:20–23a and see the glory of the Lord! This is Daniel's praise chorus right after God had intervened in a miraculous way.

Daniel believed in God's power, protection, and provision. So can you.

To close today, make Daniel's praise-chorus-prayer (Daniel 2:20–23) your own. Pause between verses to reflect and apply them to your own circumstances. Set your Stage. Expect Him.

SESSION THREE: RUN WITH TENACITY

Day Three "The Staying Power of the Dream"

I have to just stop here and catch my breath: I am just a little bit excited because this topic happens to be the core of my spirit and motivation! Dreaming big is no joke to me. God created us to be dreamers – dreamers with tenacity for when the going gets rough.

From this point forward, as we continue to grow together, I will be implementing small lessons on goals to help us believe big with a tenacious spirit. In today's work, we jump right into studying one of my favorite biblical heroes who had a tenacious spirit: Nehemiah. From the biblical account of his life and mission, we know that life is *a battle from start to finish.*

Ring a bell? Let's get started.

Remember where we were yesterday in Daniel? The Israelites were under the authority of a succession of Babylonian kings. God had ordained that His disobedient people would know the refining fire of being invaded, captured, and hauled out of Judah. The temple of Solomon was now destroyed and the Jews were in exile – far from their homeland. As we pick up at Nehemiah, King Cyrus issued a decree to allow the return of the Jews from exile. And as they began to pick through what was left of their beloved homeland, they saw nothing but rubble.

Nehemiah had a vision to rebuild the broken city, and his first goal was the walls.

> *Eliashib the high priest and his fellow priests went to work and rebuilt the Sheep Gate. They dedicated it and set its doors in place, building as far as the Tower of the Hundred, which they dedicated, and the Tower of Hananel. The men of Jericho built the adjoining section, and Zaccur son of Imri built next to them.*

The Fish Gate was rebuilt by the sons of Hassenaah. They laid its beams and put its doors and bolts and bars in place. Meremoth son of Uriah, the son of Hakkoz, repaired the next section. Next to him Mechullam son of Berekiah, the son of Mesheszabel, made repairs, and next to him Zadok son of Baana also made repairs. Nehemiah 3:1–4

Aside from the fact that these verses contain so many potential biblical names for your male children or grandchildren ("Hey, Baana-McFaana … get on in here for dinner!"), did you notice how utterly methodical this is? The work of rebuilding is portioned out and done in *pieces*. This is similar to our Run: we are in the process of learning to Run and reshape our lives. Part of the staying power of our visions and dreams *is taking one step at a time*. Or, for our purposes for today, taking one letter at a time.

DREAM

DREAM

A *dreamer* takes the "what-ifs" and puts them before God, and allows God to mold them into the desires of the heart, by His Word and His Spirit. The details of God's timing – even the final destination –may be hazy, but as we Run in faithfulness, the dream will come into focus.

And along the way, we will make some discoveries. Not all of them will be lovely.

Read Nehemiah 1:1–4.

Some of the men went ahead of Nehemiah to scout out Judah and report back. What did they find?

_____

What was Nehemiah's reaction to the news?

_____

The discovery of the ruins in Judah prompted Nehemiah to break down and weep. His next acts? He mourned, and then fasted and prayed, placing his anguish *and* his dream of rebuilding, before God. He couldn't physically see it, but his spiritual sight for what God had in store began to take shape in the midst of his prayer. Read the prayer, verses 5–11. You can see the shaping: from the holiness and might of God – to confession – to "reminding" God of God's promises (v. 9b) and the seed-dream of rebuilding and returning – to the ask.

Look up Hebrews 11:1 and write it below. _____

Like Nehemiah, we can be sure of what we hope for (because our desires are rooted in Christ), and we can be certain of what we cannot see, because we are placing our hopes and dreams into the most faithful of hands. And because we trust, we can be tenacious in our <u>deferred</u> circumstances. Nehemiah was tenacious in the face of deferred circumstances. He gathered information, he processed before Almighty God, and then he made a plan and got to it. (We will expand on this in a bit.)

Name one deferred circumstance in your life – an area where you feel like you are in a holding pattern or facing steep odds. How does your dream intersect with the deferred circumstances?

D<u>R</u>EAM

There will be *risk*.

Nehemiah faced a lot of <u>r</u>esistance in pushing forward with the dream. He would face authority issues, raw danger, real and deadly enemies, the laziness or reluctance of workers, naysayers, and political intrigue. He took the risk because he knew from walking with God that any moment of danger or uncertainty could *also* be one of great opportunity!

Read Nehemiah 2:18–20. This is the beginning of the rebuilding, and onlookers had opinions. Imagine that! What obstacles do you see in verses 18–20 that Nehemiah faced?

People don't usually wear name tags and declare themselves "mockers." The attacks are more subtle: the "helpful" criticism, the shady undermining, the questioning, the doubt throwing. Do you have mockers, ridiculers, and accusers who would derail you if they could? What sorts of words have landed on you that might fall into this category?

In verse 20, note how Nehemiah responds to opposition: *"I answered them by saying, "The God of heaven will give us success. We his servants will start rebuilding, but as for you, you have no share in Jerusalem or any claim or historic right to it."*

What can you learn about Nehemiah's character in this verse?

How will you practice this with your mockers? (Write out a sample statement.)

HINT: God sometimes removes people from your life to protect you. Don't run after them.

DR<u>E</u>AM

Nehemiah *established* goals and strategies, *brick by brick*, to help him navigate toward his dream. His first strategy was to begin well: in prayer. Earlier we touched on the pattern of Nehemiah's prayer. Now we are going to establish each brick and apply this pattern to our own prayer. Pull up a dream of yours, deferred or impossible or in process, and follow Nehemiah's example in your own words. Saying it is fine, but writing it out hones your thinking and narrows your focus. It's worth the ink.

Recognize the character of God. (Nehemiah 1:5) _____

Repent of sin, personal and corporate. (Nehemiah 1:6–7) _____

"Remind" God of His promises (Scripture). (Nehemiah 1:8–10) _____

Request specific help to begin the process. (Nehemiah 1:10–11) _____

Nehemiah ended by stating who he was. Here's who you are:

I, _____, am a daughter of the King!

DREAM

Nehemiah knew that in order for the dream to push forward, he would need others (Nehemiah 2:12). He would need *accountability*. We were not created to Run alone.

Teamwork means we train a chosen few: we share a common ideal, embrace a common goal. Regardless of any differences, we serve shoulder to shoulder, confident in one another's faith, trust, and commitment.

Another accountability option is to go public with your dream, your vision. When you communicate the vision to those in positions of authority in your life, you gain their prayers over you, their guidance, and their investment.

Do you have godly accountability in your life? (Accountability can also be found in your small group.) If not, ask God to direct you to a stronger place of accountability. We need the iron-sharpening-iron and "spurring one another on to good deeds" (Hebrews 10:24) that come with this component.

Another form of accountability is sharing your hurts with someone who is experiencing, or has experienced, the same pain. I just recently shared tears over the phone with a friend as we took our teen children to the throne room of God. Not only did we speak the same language and know the heart-hurt of what was going on in each other's families, but we also held each other accountable to Biblical standards in how we conducted ourselves in these parenting relationships. We also lifted one another, and our children, up in prayer.

DREAM

Multiply. Nehemiah presented the plan to others and encouraged them to join. He was an extraordinary leader who cast his vision and inspired others.

Then I said to them, "You see the trouble we are in: Jerusalem lies in ruins, and its gates have been burned with fire. Come, let us rebuild the wall of Jerusalem, and we will no longer be in disgrace. I also told them about the gracious hand of my God on me and what the king had said to me. They replied, "Let us start rebuilding." So they began this good work. (Nehemiah 2:17–18) (Emphasis added.)

Four distinct steps (underlined above) happened between Nehemiah's dream being something he alone owned, and the dream becoming multiplied, staffed, and completed:

1. "You see the trouble we are in …" *The need was told.*
2. "Come let us rebuild …" *A plan was given.*
3. "I also told them about the gracious hand of my God …" *Sharing the greatness of God inspired others.*
4. "Let us start rebuilding …" *They responded and joined.*

Build your "team"! Listen for the Dream … Step out, though it's risky … Establish your goals, brick by brick … Build in accountability to keep you on track … Recruit prayer warriors and laborers … *Run with it!*

Sweet dreams, Princess. The King is on your side.

SESSION THREE: RUN WITH TENACITY

Day Four "Run with *it*"

So ... what is the "*it*"?

> *Then the LORD replied: "Write down the revelation ('vision' – HCSB translation) and make it plain on tablets so that a herald may* run with it." *Habakkuk 2:2 (emphasis added.)*

God wants you to trust that He will give you a *vision* of purpose for your life, your family, your church, your city, your business, and more. Like 1 Corinthians 2:9, no eye has seen, no ear has heard, and no human mind has conceived the things that God has prepared for those who love Him!

When we seek God, we will begin to discover the *it*.

My very first pastor, Jim Combs, was a dreamer. He was so tenacious and seeking and believing that it was invigorating to be around him. I wanted to know his God. I wanted this God who had Pastor Jim so on fire. He loved examples – practical illustrations – that brought the biblical concepts to life. Here is one that still, after all these years, is one of my favorites.

When you go camping, you bring with you all the equipment and can't wait for the bonfire. And when it is time to turn in, you crawl into your tent to go to sleep. But sleeping in a tent at night obstructs the view of the stars. Your view of the beauty and majesty and splendor of the heavens is obscured. Many times we have things in the way that obstruct God's visions and splendor for our lives. Sometimes we think to crawl out and look up. Sometimes God brings people into our lives to open up our tent flaps and invite us to go on deeper walks with Him. I had a little of both. And it is when I stepped out of my tent that the real journey started and I began to see the stars.

This may be the most important chapter for me personally. Reflecting back to the beginning stages of my spiritual learning and growth, I realize that God took each act, each brick, to deposit His dreams into my heart, and then began to breathe life into them. This Bible study is a dream come true! What I am sharing today works. Let's now go after what is already inside of you.

We are heading to Habakkuk. Habakkuk predicted and warned about the invasion of Judah by the Chaldeans. (This was the ethnic group rose to power and eventually became known as the Babylonians. Sound familiar?) Much of Habakkuk is specific to the prophesy, and reading it will give shimmers of Job. Like Job, Habakkuk struggles with understanding God's ways and longs to discern God's purposes in the midst of this world. We know from the totality of scripture that God's desire is for us to live abundantly, in joy, security, and righteousness. Our question becomes, "How do we discern this as individuals?"

Habakkuk's interaction with God (much like Job's) is a back-and-forth of questions and answers. We can learn from Habakkuk's interaction with the sovereign God. God does not always give clear answers to the questions we have, but He will call on us to be faithful: to Him, and to His purposes for our lives.

Read Habakkuk 1:1–4 below. (Habakkuk means "embrace.")

How long, Lord, must I call for help, but you do not listen? Or cry out to you, "Violence!" but you do not save? Why do you make me look at injustice? Why do you tolerate wrongdoing? Destruction and violence are before me; there is strife, and conflict abounds. Therefore, the law is paralyzed, and justice never prevails. The wicked hem in the righteous so that justice is perverted. (Habakkuk 1:1–4)

Now put on your cranky pants and let's get down to business.

This section of Habakkuk is known as his "First Prayer" in some translations, and as "Habakkuk's Complaint" in the NIV. That's more accurate, don't you think? As he offers his opinions to God about the conditions of his world, Habakkuk then asks some tough questions.

Your turn. In the considerable space below, give it a shot, modeling Habakkuk: complain, lament, purge, express what confuses you or frustrates you. Then ask, ask, ask the hard questions of God. (It's okay. This is a safe place.)

And if you are in a season of celebration right now, recall sometime in the past when concerns led you to ask some tough questions.

What is the promise given to us in this scripture? _____

Look back at your complaints. Do you sense God's movement in any of those areas? _____

It is sometimes hard to wrap our minds around things when we are coming through losses or very crippling situations. Please try, little by little, to break out of the setback. When we allow our minds to be renewed and remember who He is and that He is always at work around us, we open ourselves up to the possibility of a breakthrough. We start to notice a star peeking out right there ... and over there.

Read Habakkuk 2:2–3. The Lord's answer: "Look at the nations and watch – and be utterly amazed. For I am going to do something in your days that you would not believe, even if you were told." (Habakkuk 1:5)

Habakkuk goes through a second complaint (verses 12–14) and is angry, tormented, and accusatory. He even goes so far as to correct God. And then ... and then ... he braces for God's response. It is such an abrupt departure that it's almost like he puts himself in a timeout. Habakkuk clears his throat, pulls back his emotion, and positions himself to hear from God, with eagerness.

Read Habakkuk 2:1 and then use the questions to assess your own positioning.

I will stand at my watch and station myself on the ramparts; I will look to see what He will say to me, and what answer I am to give to this complaint. (Habakkuk 2:1)

Many times we spin out of control and run in all directions. In this verse Habakkuk decides to *wait, watch,* and *listen,* and learns to Run in Such A Way.

How are you taking positive action to wait, watch, and listen? How can you regroup and calm your sweet self down? _____

The Lord's answer:

Then the Lord replied: "Write down the revelation and make it plain on tablets so that a herald may run with it. For the revelation awaits an appointed time; it speaks of the end and will not prove false. Though it linger, wait for it; it will certainly come and will not delay." (Habakkuk 2:2–3)

And we have come full circle.

For what fresh revelation are you waiting? _____

In this week's "The Extra Lap," we will go into detail about journaling, because right now you're thinking, "I don't have any extra stone tablets next to my highlighter markers ..." and "What in the world do I write?" and "Why does it even matter?"

For now, to close out today, recite Habakkuk 3:16–19 (below), and think about the complaints you may have written down, the starbursts you hope to see, the fresh revelation you so desperately need. Then remember a sovereign Lord who laid the foundations of the earth, who placed the stars in the sky to draw you out of the tent, and who promises that *"it"* is on its way, in His time, in His way, but *it* is a sure thing.

Worship.

I heard and my heart pounded, my lips quivered at the sound; decay crept into my bones, and my legs trembled. Yet I will wait patiently for the day of calamity to come on the nation invading us. Though the fig tree does not bud and there are no grapes on the vines, though the olive crop fails and the fields produce no food, though there are no sheep in the pen and no cattle in the stalls, yet I will rejoice in the Lord, I will be joyful in God my Savior. The Sovereign Lord is my strength; he makes my feet like the feet of a deer, he enables me to do on the heights. (Habakkuk 3:16–19)

Mile Marker

Anita

I was born a nobody. A nothing by worldly standards. I grew
up in the shadow lands of addiction and dysfunction. I didn't
stand a chance. The odds were stacked against me.

I watched my father die from addiction when I was 11
years old, followed by my mother when I was 18.
I knew at a very early age what the devil looked
like, and I didn't want to live in that hell.

I married my knight in shining armor at 22. I never saw his rusty
armor. After eight years of marriage, he confessed his own demons.
Drugs had hijacked my family without my ever seeing it coming.

I couldn't sleep, breathe, or eat. I had these two young children and what
I thought was a perfect little family. My world came crashing down.
What I didn't know was that my life was just crumbling in place.

There were only a couple of things that were concrete in
my life at that time: my running, and my God.

I knew how to run and I knew how to pray.

Many days I needed a voice bigger than my own. The only place I
could hear God's voice was through heavy breathing and my feet

hitting the pavement. Most of the time I would pull my boys in a
Radio Flyer wagon while I was running through the neighborhoods.

On many runs I shed tears down my routes. I desperately tried
to find direction and understanding. I fell in love with my runs.
As my miles increased, my passion for running also developed.
It became more than therapy. It became a relationship.

In the span of three years my body got beat up by uncontrollable
circumstances: I had three surgeries in that time period, two of them
ACL surgeries. These really had me questioning my purpose in running.

But God never took that passion away from me.

After weeks and months of recovery and prayer, I laced my shoes back up.

God brought me back, strong and faster than ever.

Call unto me and seek me, and I will show you great *and*
mighty *things which thou knowest not. (Jeremiah 33:3)*

One day, after running three hours, I looked at my times. I'd never had
any desire to run a marathon; however, I had not only just run 20 miles –
I had also run 20 miles fast enough to qualify for the Boston Marathon.

A seed had been planted.

I qualified for Boston, and ran my first marathon in
Chicago just a few weeks later. It was 90 degrees.

I ran Boston in 2011. In 2013, I ran the Boston Marathon again. I
finished 40 minutes before the tragic events that unfolded at that
year's Boston Marathon. The bombings terrorized my family. I
had many fears, but I had to return to Boston in 2014. My family
supported my decision to return to honor the victims and finish my

Boston experience with joy and victory. Putting my fears behind me, I clung to God's promises: I let my faith in Him direct me.

God has given me the gift of running, and has used it to glorify His name.

I use my running as part of my testimony to be a witness to others. I remind others that no matter your circumstances in life, if you never quit, but instead seek God, *He will show you great and mighty things.*

SESSION THREE: RUN WITH TENACITY

Day Five "Personal Running Log"

Pace yourself

Review the week's work: the scripture you have covered, the writings on the lines and in the margins. What would you ask God for this day? What did you not quite get this week? How can you serve Him more? Who and what should you be praying for?

P Pray.
A Ask for God's vision for your life.
C Communicate back to God.
E Enter His Race for your life.

Run free in the space below: _____

Recovery questions

***What main thing did the study push me to *do, be,* or *feel* as a result of the material?

***What did God say to me through this week?

***How is my Run measuring up to this word? What action(s) will I take to bring my life in line with the word/message received this week?

My challenge

With what truth do I need to study and Train harder?

BLISTER:

"Ouch and Pinch": Jot down those moments this week that caused pain.

BLISS:

"Praise You and Thank You": Jot down your praises.

Team Spirit/Sharing Challenge: Think of someone you know who is limping right now. _____

Pray for them.
Look for an opportunity to share with them what you have learned this week.

Theme verse:

Do you not know that in a race all the runners run, but only one gets the prize? Run in such a way as to get the prize. Everyone who competes in the games goes into strict training. They do it to get a crown that will not last; but we do it to get a crown that will last forever. Therefore, I do not run like a man running aimlessly; I do not fight like a man beating the air. No, I beat my body and make it my slave so that after I have preached to others, I myself will not be disqualified for the prize. (1 Corinthians 9:24–27)

Write out the verses in the space below.

Pray the verses back to God, making them personal.

When you've memorized them, share the verses by speaking them out loud to your small group! Great job!

The Extra Lap

*On Day Four of this week's work, we learned that God told Habakkuk that
the vision must be written down.*

And on tablets.

*And maybe you're thinking: "The idea of writing down my
'vision' is as antiquated as stone tablets."*

Not so fast, Sister!

Today, we're going to look elsewhere in Scripture for information on journaling
and vision-casting.

Why journal?

Look up Deuteronomy 6:20 and write it below.

Look up Deuteronomy 32:7 and write it below.

Why might records of journaling be helpful?

Journaling is not just for remembering events of the past. Writing things down can help you narrow your focus, establish your goals, hone your prayers. For our vision purposes, you need to know that *something powerful happens when you verbalize a goal*, whether in a conversation or a journal. Putting a dream or a vision into words (written or spoken) is an act of *faith*. When you write the thing down, it holds you accountable: You can go back and say *"it is written"* in your best Morgan Freeman voice, and remember that it is there, and return to praying over it and offer it up. And you know what? It helps you remember you asked God for it! So many times we miss out on celebrating answered prayer because we forgot we asked the question!

How to journal?

This is up to you. Some keep electronic logs. Some love a good college-ruled spiral notebook. Some purchase leather-bound, gold-embossed frou-frou journals. Some write things in the margins of their Bibles, or on scraps that go into folders. You can write in phrases, code names (for sensitive issues), or elaborate in great detail. You can keep a list of what you're grateful for. You can record scriptures that "popped" on you and why.

For this lesson, we are asking that you *write down* what you hear from God about the call on your life, what you are asking Him for specifically, and date the thing. Just start. See what happens.

What is a vision, anyway?

When the Lord restored the fortunes of Zion, we were like those who dream. (Psalm 126:1)

There is a strong biblical basis for vision-casting. The context of this Psalm is the hope of the Israelites for prosperity and peace upon their return from Babylonian exile. They were straggling back into a decimated Jerusalem and an uncertain future. Dare they hope? Did they feel silly because they were "realists", and did they try to push down any hopeful wishes that kept popping up? Did they whisper? Or did they *declare* the hope?

The commentary on this verse says that "like those who dream" refers to those *who eagerly anticipate the future.*

Anticipate the future! *Write it down.*

Dream big: *Write it down.*

Think about "what could be if ..." *Write it down.*

Consider your passions, gifts, and season of life, and wonder before a mighty God: *Write it down.*

Prayer and imagination are directly proportional; free your imagination from the chains of being a "realist" ... then pray more and see your tent flaps fly open! *Write it down.*

If you have no idea what to write down, ask the Holy Spirit to help you. Wait. Watch. And when something "occurs" to you: *Write it down.*

When a portion of scripture shimmers on you, and there's something in there for you but you can't quite put your finger on it: *Write it down.*

When someone in your world says something that echoes what you just prayed over that morning:

Write it down.

Get the picture?

Nothing honors God more than a big dream that is way beyond our ability to accomplish. I'll bet you know why, right? Because when something is bigger than we understand or can even see clearly, we are in raw dependence on the super-sizing, wonder-filling miracle-worker God, and it is *God* who gets the *glory!*

SESSION FOUR

Runner's Roadblocks

1 CORINTHIANS 9: 24–27

Do you not know that in a race all the runners run, but only one gets the prize? Run in such a way as to get the prize. Everyone who competes in the games goes into strict training. They do it to get a crown that will not last; but we do it to get a crown that will last forever. Therefore, I do not run like a man running aimlessly; I do not fight like a man beating the air. No, I beat my body and make it my slave so that after I have preached to others, I myself will not be disqualified for the prize.

SESSION FOUR: LECTURE NOTES

SESSION FOUR: RUNNER'S ROADBLOCKS

The Warm-up

Without warning, something can rise up and bring you down. Just like *that*. Quick as lightning.

And now your timeline has a hash mark: *This* happened *then*. From that hash mark forward, the world has a different hue, and is forever marked by the indentation of that knifepoint.

****

One afternoon I was sitting on the couch, bawling my eyes out. I cried until I had that "cry headache," if you know what I mean. I sobbed like a big baby girl because my life had just been turned upside-down. I had discovered something secret: my husband was involved with another woman. I had suspected something for several months (which is a whole 'nother round of anxiety), but on this particular day, the secret had been spilled through an accidental message on a pager.

> *The righteous cry out, and the Lord hears them; He delivers them from all their troubles. The Lord is close to the brokenhearted and saves those who are crushed in spirit."* (Psalm 34:17–19)

I was nine months pregnant with my second child at the time, and my son was three years old. I was torn to pieces, sick to my stomach, lifeless.

> *In this world you will have trouble. But take heart: I have overcome the world.* (John 16:33)

The adversity in my marriage and the struggles with my husband have humbled me and softened my heart. As I grew toward God, I learned to cherish His ways and depend on Him for everything.

> *The suffering you sent was good for me, for it taught me to pay attention to your principles. Psalm 119:71 (New Living Translation)*

I went through the devastation and restoration of my marriage, and it was a long and hard path. And now I have a knowledge of something that women don't have until they go through it. I am more compassionate, I know what not to say, and I know to hold onto it until the "cry headache" has passed. God has had me use my hurt and my healing over and over again to help others.

> *Praise be to the God and Father of our Lord Jesus Christ, the Father of compassion and the God of all comfort, who comforts us in all our troubles, so that we can comfort those in any trouble … For just as the sufferings of Christ flow over into our lives, so also through Christ, our comfort overflows. (2 Corinthians 1:3–5)*

****

So, one of my stories is the story of my marriage. That may not be your story, but perhaps the loss or illness of a loved one? Your own illness? A promising career cut short? Addictions, afflictions?

Children who walk away from God? The press of relentless financial worries? Roadblocks, all.

So what's a Runner to do? This is our focus this week. Because God has a purpose and a plan, and not one big-girl tear is wasted because our God is always good.

> *So take a new grip with your tired hands and stand firm on your shaky legs. Mark out a straight path for your feet. Then those who follow you, though they are weak and lame, will not stumble and fall, but will become strong. (Hebrews 12:12–13) (New Living Translation)*

SESSION FOUR: RUNNER'S ROADBLOCKS

Day One "Shin Splints and Stress Fractures"

Shin splints (noun): A *painful condition* of the front lower leg, associated with tendinitis, muscle *strain* …

Stress fracture (noun): a *fatigue fracture* of the bone caused by repeated application of a *heavy load*, such as the *constant pounding* on a surface by runners, gymnasts, and dancers …

The general definitions of today's terms came neither with underscored, eye-catching relevance, nor in boldface. But if you've ever had either? You know they warrant the *bold*. And take a look at the descriptors: painful condition … strain … fatigue fracture … heavy load … constant pounding … Oh. Yes.

In the Run of our life, a heart fracture can trigger a profound spiritual struggle. We can question why God would allow us to be laid up in physical and emotional pain, and unless we learn to deal faithfully and effectively with the roadblocks, and accept them as allowed by the hand of God, our Runs will be reduced to putting one bitter foot in front of the other – that is, if we are able to move at all.

Look up Hebrews 12:1 and write it below.

If you used the NIV translation (or a few others), you would have written, "The sin that so easily entangles." Of course the sin so easily entangles. Let's round the bases and bring it home:

Imagine attempting a marathon with your shoelaces tied together.

Can you see how slow the progress would be?

How far could you reasonably run without tripping and falling over? Repeatedly?

Imagine the frustration of the same knee getting skinned … again.

After a while, wouldn't you want to just roll over and give up?

How many people have you seen get tripped up in their Christian Races over bitterness, lying, jealousy, idolatry, addiction, sexual sin, anger, promiscuity, fear, failure? After a while, we can start to buy into the tangle and disqualify ourselves from the Race completely!

Back to Hebrews 12:1. In the New Living Translation, the "throw off every hindrance" is swapped for "strip off every weight." Doesn't that seem meatier? Don't you want to stop lugging the bag of rocks you've been carrying around? Doesn't that seem more urgent than the shrugging off of a hindrance?

So let's lose some weight.

The story of Elijah in 1 Kings 18 is one of the best examples of a God-powered encounter in the Bible. It is Elijah at Mount Carmel, standing up to King Ahab and the prophets of Baal and, in the mighty name of the One True Almighty God, calling down Yahweh's fire and rain to declare the sovereignty of the Lord. And then, as Ahab is in a chariot hustling to Jezreel, the power of the Lord comes onto Elijah, and Elijah *outruns the chariot and beats Ahab to Jezreel.*

Does this supernatural fireworks extravaganza and miraculous work bring about the repentance of God's people, and turn them from false idols?

Nope.

At least not in a measurable-enough way to warrant ink in scripture.

And then Ahab's wife, Queen Jezebel, sends out mercenaries to murder Elijah. He is on the run. So Elijah collapses into an almost-hysterical pessimism. He is physically and emotionally exhausted, fearful, despondent.

The weight of despair:

Has something shattered your focus and faith? What problems are you running from?

_____

In 1 Kings 19:3–5, we find Elijah landing near Beersheba (which belonged to Judah and was a safe territory) and leaving his servant behind. He heads into the wilderness and prays; he asks God to take him Home, since he feels like a failure. Elijah cries out to God: "I have had enough … Take my life."

The weight of failure and exhaustion:

Have you ever felt like Elijah, thinking, "I just can't do this anymore"? In what ways are you exhausted?

_____

In 1 Kings 19:5–7, Elijah falls asleep under a tree, and then an angel awakens him, saying, "Get up and eat." There is a loaf of warm bread and a jug of water, and he eats and drinks. Elijah sleeps, and the same sequence happens again, with the angel saying, "Arise, eat, because the journey (to come) is too great for you."

The weight-lifting of an encourager:

Have you ever been encouraged by someone when you were down and out?

_____

Who can you encourage by bringing some "angel-food cake"?

We are turning a corner here, *from Elijah's shin splints and stress fractures to the tending, healing, and sending of God. This is our blueprint.*

Elijah then walks 40 days and 40 nights, arriving at a cave and taking shelter there. And Elijah and God enter into conversation in which Elijah gets to air it all out. (1 Kings 19:9–14)

The weight-lifting of venting to God

Sometimes when we feel alone and abandoned, God can do His best work in us. In your cave, licking your wounds? Vent to God. He can take it, and will set your heart – and your feet – aright.

The weight-lifting of purpose and direction

In I Kings 19:15, God gives Elijah something to do. Elijah needed to lift his head from his circumstances and despair, and get on with what God wanted him to do.

Has God given you something to do recently that you have avoided?

After Elijah did God's bidding, Elisha was appointed as his successor, and the "ceremony" played out like this: Elijah walked past Elisha and "threw his mantle over him." Done.

The Hebrew word for mantle is "addereth" (literally, "prophet's garment"), but has come to symbolize one's calling in the Kingdom of God and the authority that the calling necessitates. *You* have a mantle. Your mantle is ageless. Your mantle was decided before you were born. As you Run your Race, who might have taught you, guided you, into knowing your gifts and leanings? The garment is being handed to you: are you going to put it on? Are you going to accept the anointing that comes with a God-designed plan for your life? That "hunch", or "inkling", that God might be asking of you? What if that was the key?

Untangle your laces and hit the road. Your step is lighter now. Your heavy load has been transferred in a "ceremony" known as Calvary: His sacrifice, love, provision, and healing. Come on, now … You were Born to Run*!*

SESSION FOUR: RUNNER'S ROADBLOCKS

Day One "The Wall"

I have to share this story.

In 2013, my husband and I were training for the Detroit Marathon, which was coming up in October. We've run a lot of races together (most of them not marathons!), as it is a sport we enjoy together. We don't really run to be competitive; we run to keep in shape, for the mutual discipline and accountability, and because we enjoy it. Since we had run marathons before, and knew what to expect and how to prepare, we were pretty serious about training – mostly to eliminate or lessen the chance of hitting "the wall" at whatever mile.

One beautiful July morning, I set out alone for a four-mile training run. Since that distance was, by now, pretty easy for me, I decided to spice it up with some fast sprints along the path. During one of my sprints, I "gracefully" tripped and fell hard. A face-plant in the cement, crunching my right knee in the process. Oh, but my sisters, let me tell you the best part: where I fell was along the main busy street right before I would turn into my subdivision. I knew a lot of people passing in cars had seen me go down, so you know what I did? I made it look like I was an elite athlete by going right into push-ups.

Oh, yes, I made my fall look intentional – as though I had planned to sprint right into the push-ups! (Don't judge me!)

I sure looked tough and strong doing push-ups on the main road in front of millions – while in serious pain. After awhile, I s-l-o-w-l-y got up and ran in pain to hide behind Walgreens. I just stood in silence, looking at my scraped-up knee and ripped running pants.

I was a hot, hot mess. Not seeing the obstacle/wall/uneven pavement brought me pain and took from me the marathon I had been training for.

A wall can suggest a barrier to your movement in life, but it can also symbolize protection. Boundaries are healthy for protection, but barriers can stop you from Running your Race. Many times barriers are formed around our hearts due to hurt from the past. Let's compare healthy walls to insurmountable barriers.

There are two kinds of walls:

Toxic walls that are barriers *and* Life-giving walls of protection

This is especially true when we are Running our spiritual Races. We need to know how to discern between good walls and bad walls.

A Wall that Must Come Down: Hard-Heartedness

Look up Hebrews 3:15 and write it below.

_____

In Hebrews 3:15, the writer is referring back to the strong words of Psalm 95. In this Psalm, the disobedience of the Israelites in the wilderness is judged harshly: they do not get to enter the Promised Land because they have hardened their hearts against God. In their rebellion, they neither pay any heed to God's Word nor obey God's commands.

If you read and wrote down Hebrews 3:15, you *are* hearing His voice. Be alert and on guard, and apply the antidote: *Read Ezekiel 36:26–27.*

What are the steps for the "heart transplant"?

Where do you sense hard-heartedness? How might the "transplant" play out in this area of your life?

A Wall that Must Come Down: Double-Mindedness

This wall can go up very fast when we try to integrate things of this world with the promises and conditions of God's Word. (James 1:8)

Read Romans 8:5–8. What do these verses mean to you?

Romans 8:7 tells us that this is not a peaceful coexistence we have with the ways of the world. Trying to keep one foot in each camp is futile and ugly. The world is hostile to the ways of God, and when we allow ourselves to determine our days by our sinful nature, we *cannot* please God.

***Quickly: when you read those last sentences, what "uh-oh" situation/area of your life sprang to mind?

A Wall that Must Come Down: Lack of Faith

We could talk a lot about lack of faith, but in this context, think of lack of faith as the bottom, the foundational layer of the wall. From that beginning, we can build all kinds of nasty. Lack of faith leads to doubt, fear, defeat, exhaustion, wasting your time and energy by Running in the wrong direction, emotional paralysis, or disengaging from God's Word or God's people. Left in place, these are huge barriers to your Run and to your abundant life.

All because of misplaced faith.

We decide to believe what our eyes can see in our natural selves, rather than what God tells us is *real*. We often choose to Run headlong into a brick wall. We actually choose the injury and the bleeding because we decide not to listen to God when He tells us it is there.

What follows is Jen's story in this session's Mile Marker. Her story is about the day her heart was crushed and her life was forever marked. She could have misplaced her faith in her moment of crisis and grief, but thankfully, her story was covered by Jesus.

Mile Marker

Jen

It was exactly three weeks before the accident that I read the book *The Shack*. *The Shack* is a very popular Christian book based on a question of faith after a family tragedy. Most of my Christian friends had read the book years earlier. The book touched me in a way I'll never forget. Immediately after reading it, I was referring it to all my friends and family to read, most of whom already had. There was a particular part of the story that stood out to me. The main character, Mack, has a discussion with Jesus, and he asks why his daughter was all alone with her abductor. Jesus explains in the story that she was never alone, that Jesus was with her the whole time, and that they talked, and that his daughter was brave and at peace and even prayed for her family during that time.

That brings me to June 29, 2010. *This was the day my own personal family tragedy began.*

I was frantically called to the scene of a single-car accident, in which my 18-year-old son was a front-seat passenger in a car that had collided at a very high rate of speed into a tree. The scene was blocked off and had me several feet away, and friends and family gathered in fear for the three boys in that car. The ambulance was leaving and the helicopter was taking off, and many were following these vehicles to the hospital. However, my son, Brad, was not on his way to the hospital. For him the accident had been fatal, and I was told they were doing their best to get out him of that car as quickly as they could, but literally hours passed.

I was in shock. I couldn't believe what was happening. He had just graduated from high school and had his whole life ahead of him. He was a son, a grandson, an older brother, a nephew, a cousin, and a friend to so many. His best friend of 10 years had been driving … this just couldn't be happening. It couldn't be *real*; it felt like a complete nightmare. The reality started to slowly sink in after hours of waiting, and I was forced to realize that this *was* real – my worst fear, and any parent's worst nightmare.

It was actually happening.

As the news media, friends, and family came and left, I stood there, brokenhearted, and yet couldn't leave with the others. I couldn't leave the scene before my son did. I will never forget standing there, alone, crying out to God. I asked God, *Why?* Not *Why me?* but rather, *Why was Brad in that car now, all alone?* Why couldn't I get closer to him? Why couldn't I be there to tell him it was all going to be okay? Or to tell him that I loved him? It was at that moment that the story of Mack's conversation with Jesus came flashing back to me. It was then that, I swear to this day, I felt a light squeeze on my shoulders from behind, and heard (spoken to me? or in my heart?):

"He's not alone; I am right there with him."

Nobody could convince me that it wasn't part of God's plan for me to read that book, for me to be so touched by it, in preparation for my own worst nightmare.

God has promised through his Word to comfort those who mourn.

Since then, God has done just that for me. My faith has grown in ways that are hard to describe. Comforting a mother who grieves for her son is a God-sized job. There have been so many stories in my life, such as this one, that have shown God to be faithful. I believe that once you believe that God is faithful to his word,

and you Run to him, you'll be more open to see just how good
he his! He sends comfort in many different forms, whether:

... it's a butterfly (or "Brad-erfly", as I would call it),

... a bird,

... a song,

... a verse,

... a kind word from a stranger,

... a hug from a loved one.

... One way or another, God shows Himself to be
faithful, and He continues to bring me comfort.

I wouldn't have survived my dark night of the soul without my faith or
my God. I am so very thankful that it continues to grow every day.

Jen says her faith is stronger than it has ever been, and that she can do all things through God's strength! Jen understands that God is stronger and bigger than death and her grief. She did not let the wall become a barrier – she tore the thing down, brick by brick. And scaled the wall. And let God scoop her up and lift her over.

Do you struggle with the Wall of Lack of Faith?

Can you identify an occasion when God turned what you were enduring around so that you could help another through a similar tragedy or circumstance or diagnosis?

A Wall that Must Go Up and Stay Up

It seems like for the past three years I have been standing at the same wall. I stand in front and say to myself, "I need to get past this wall." I tend to …

- Doubt my calling
- Doubt at times that I am in the right church
- Feel inadequate or that I have not *dispensed* my giftings effectively

You don't want to quit when you *hit* the wall! You want to continue to dream and serve, but at the same time desire new, fresh movement. But you feel stuck at a wall, wondering if you are missing new levels of knowledge, new levels of failure, or new levels of wisdom. The wall seems to have different texture depending on what you are dealing with in that season. For example:

- the wall of no events
- the wall of book publishing difficulty
- the wall of going broke for your dream
- the wall of dream discouragement

Jeremiah 29:11 states, "For I know the plans I have for you, declares the Lord!" (So personal while at our walls!) "Plans to prosper you and not to harm you. Plans to give you a hope and a future." Friends, when we stand at a wall for a long time, we tend to get confused about whether to stay and deal with any problems or sin we may have, or to leave and look for the *"new."* Many times the silence at the wall is a time of personal pruning. We have to realize that God is faithful and often we need to remain at the wall. *Do not become disillusioned* by the lack of events at this time or season at the wall.

Runners … when we get stuck during a tough mile, often we feel like we have hit that wall. It's okay to stop and stand still before that wall and let your spirit *Run in prayer.* I love Psalm 25:4–5:

"Show me Your ways, O Lord; teach me Your path. Lead me in Your Truth and teach me. For You are the God of my salvation, and on You I will wait." (*Yes*, you will wait at your wall all day.) Waiting, but Running in Spirit and Truth.

This is so very important... Remember, the wall can become your biggest blessing in time. Learn and grow as you wait, watch, and listen at that wall. Do you feel disillusioned at a wall at this time? Please write out Psalm 25 above and get ready to be alert for how God is going to intervene at that wall. _____

Look up Isaiah 49:16 and write it below. _____

The wording of this passage tells us that God has *you* engraved in the palm of His hands. He has placed you within His grip, the center of His strength. And then look at the words that follow – our walls are continually before Him. What does this mean?

This refers to Jerusalem's *defensive* walls. In ancient times, walled cities were important.

– Walls helped in resisting enemies, and often deterred attacks.
– In a city that went dark at night, walls kept its inhabitants from wandering into danger.
– Walls also kept livestock enclosed and protected: a wall protected financial well-being.

So how might this play out in our Race? Proverbs 25:28 declares that "a person without self-control is like a city with broken-down walls." God wants to keep us safe by putting up *boundaries*, walls of *protection*, so that His children are kept safe from the Enemy, from attacks, from thieves, from getting lost, from wandering off. It's our choice, of course. God always gives us freedom. We can choose to live in the safety of His strong and loving grip and oversight and protection, or we can kick a hole in the wall and give the Enemy easy access.

Want some scary reading? Read Ezekiel 22:25–30.

Oh, friends. Aren't there days when the evil prowling on our planet seems like a hungry lion licking its chops, about ready to pounce on the stragglers, the unprotected, the vulnerable, your family?

Do you have a wall to keep the enemies of God out of your life and home? If not, which walls to you need to erect?

If you do have a wall, are you leaving the gates open and unguarded? Are you willing to fight the enemy, or let the enemy stream in unchallenged? What does that look like in practice – how to you stand your guard?

As you close today, ask God to direct your thoughts to gates you might have accidentally left open. Ask for His supernatural defense against the enemy, a hedge of protection, so that you can Run in safety.

SESSION FOUR: RUNNER'S ROADBLOCKS

Day Three "Knots so Good"

But those who hope in the Lord will renew their strength.
They will soar on wings like eagles; they will run and
not grow weary, they will walk and not be faint.
(Isaiah 40:31)

Do you ever suffer from Race anxiety? Anxiety changes the way you think. Sometimes it can make you think more negatively. Sometimes it can make you obsess over things you shouldn't obsess over. And sometimes anxiety can cause your thoughts to spin out of control. Racing, rapid, disconnected thoughts can make you feel like you're going a little crazy!

This came straight out of the mouth of a woman in my small group one morning: "When running crazy on the hamster wheel of life, things accumulate. In the midst of everything, all the emotions take over and we fly off the wheel. Ever seen a hamster fly off the wheel? We have to learn how to Run it out … in other words, do our pity-party dance in a healthy way!"

If you push through the all those emotions, push through the physical exhaustion, push through the spiritual roadblocks, push through the relational chaos … (I'm tired just *writing* this …) You come to the end of your rope feeling "knots so good".

Almost every physical runner experiences pre-race jitters or performance anxiety. As their performance improves, the runner will often put *more* pressure on themselves rather than relax into their stride. The same can be true with our spiritual Race: we can become so consumed by the Finish Line and whether are we on pace with the others. And, oh, my goodness, we feel defeated, rejected, and pushed over the edge, and … at the end of our ropes.

On my father's side of the family, suicide hunts and haunts. The tragedies have left me shaken and changed.

—   My dad's sister took her life when relationship problems and pain and medication addictions overwhelmed her weary soul.
—   My dad's brother overdosed – a slow suicide of addiction and temptation.
—   My dad's other brother took his life in a garage when the weight of his life became a burden that was too heavy.
—   My dad's nephew – my cousin – took his life when marriage and finances and self-medicating became too much. I spoke at my cousin's funeral and looked out and saw the agony in the faces and hearts of my family. It was gut-wrenching.
—   And just recently my dad spoke to me of the first suicide he had memory of: his own grandmother. I knew of the others, but not this one. The knowledge froze me in my tracks.

So many loved ones who came to the end of their ropes. I have spent years pondering this loss of hope.

This is not God's design for us – this ongoing, relentless, suffocating despair has no place in the abundant life. I've spent years studying scripture and reaching out to other women who grieve like me. We look at our sick and long for their healing. We hurt for them because the darkness encroaches, and we pray specific blessings on those who yet grieve. We whisper prayers of protection over our children and for a hedge around our minds, that our thoughts will not get tangled, and we seek the Giver of Hope who is Lord of All.

We have to learn how to Run in Such A Way in our broken world. We are not without hope.

I have told you these things so that in me you may have peace. In this world you will have trouble. But take heart! I have overcome the world. (John 16:33)

Heal me, O Lord, and I will be healed; save me and I will be saved, for you are the one I praise. (Jeremiah 17:14)

"For I know the plans I have for you," declares the Lord, "plans to prosper you and not to harm you, plans to give you hope and a future." (Jeremiah 29:11)

"Christ in you is the hope of glory." Colossians 1:27 (emphasis added)

This is not going to be a place where Bible verses are thrown at you, and you are kissed on the top of your head and sent on your way. Suicide, depression, and mental illness are very serious and often tragic circumstances to navigate personally and as a family.

In 2013, five days after Easter, Matthew Warren took his own life. He was the son of Rick and Kay Warren (Saddleback Church). Said Kay:

"Following Matthew's death I felt like I was sitting on the edge of Hell. Romans 5 tells us that His hope does not disappoint us. Well, I wasn't disappointed – I was crushed. It felt like my life had been reduced to ashes. But God is not helpless among the ruins; he continues to work out his plan in love. Where there is ruining in your life, God rebuilds."

Since their family's tragedy, the couple has sponsored and advocated open discussions on how God's Church can come alongside those who have mental illness and those who have loved ones with mental illness. God is using their story to rebuild from the ruins.

If this is an issue you are currently suffering, God's Church can come alongside you and offer care and direction and help. Please let your small group leader – or someone on staff – know of your need. Our fallen world keeps falling apart, and even though as God's people we can't fix the world, we can show up to support each other and look up to the One who heals and redeems.

Could we pause for a moment right here and pray? *Father, please be with families that have suffered sudden losses and losses of loved ones. Comfort them with hope in the midst of their darkest despair. Guide all of our families, Lord, in the midst of shame and pain and confusion and forgiveness. Surround us with Your presence, Your love, Your goodness, and a hope the world cannot understand. Amen.*

Most of us will confront hopelessness on a lesser level. At the time, it won't feel "lesser" to us, of course! The failures, hurts, and hard events of our lives will try to strangle the *spiritual* life right out of us.

For the remainder of today's lesson, we're going to look at how God's Word gives us the prescription for that kind of Healing.

Here's a baseline for you: *We prejudge our situations, and misjudge God's actions in them… and then we get all tied up in knots over it.*

Isn't this truer than you want to think? Oh, but we can conjecture and conjure and get it *all wrong* in our teeny-tiny human brains!

> *Trust in the Lord with all your heart and lean not on your own understanding.*
> *In all your ways, acknowledge him, and he will make your paths straight.*
> *Proverbs 3:5–6*

So, if our ability to fully understand is compromised by our humanity, and if the mystery of *all* that God is and does is not available to us, and we know that God is *good*, why do we have trust issues in our circumstances and hardships? Who is that whispering sweet awful things into our ears?

We have an enemy who is a liar. Let's look at some of Satan's most useful knots. Circle the knots you may need to untangle.

1. *In your comprehension and understanding of God.*

   Satan will tell you that God is mad at you, that God will not forgive you because you've really gone too far this time, and that it is *way* too late to recover. Satan will tell you that you are a hypocrite and that God will never have a use for you.

   None of this is true! God sees you through the sacrifice and victory of Jesus Christ, and looks at you through eyes of compassion and goodness and mercy. It is *not* too late. Failure is *not* final. God is not willing that any should perish, and longs for you to "come home" into the shelter of His arms and know His peace and joy. The Father quite simply *adores* you.

   Deception with self

   – "You are no good."
   – "Aren't you *ever* going to get this?"

- "You're a loser and everyone knows it."
- "You'll never amount to anything ..."
- "Would anyone even notice if you left the room?"
- "No one is proud of you or any of your 'accomplishments.'"

Satan loves to sow seeds of self-doubt and accusation and cause us to devalue our worth in Christ. It's one of his most reliable parlor tricks, mostly because it continues to work like a charm. We fall for it. So, just as Satan would love to ensnare us with lies about the goodness of God, it's a double win if he can also convince us of our worthlessness *to* God!

Read John 8:44. As Jesus is emphatically describing those who follow Satan (this section is often categorized as "Children of the Devil"), he underscores that Satan is not only a liar, but also a murderer. Why would you listen to anything a liar and a murderer have to say?

2. *Satan will try to get to us through others.*

Satan tries to bring shame against you because of things others have done to you. Abuse victims often carry deep-rooted shame around with them. Victims of misplaced trust feel like fools. Victims of gossip or bullying want to cower in the corner. Some days, it can take just a "funny look" from someone or a rude remark, and we're pretty sure we deserved it because we have believed Satan's lies about us.

Let's be honest: Satan has lots of willing accomplices running through your neighborhood and workplace. People will intentionally hurt you. People will unintentionally hurt you. Because you belong to Christ, do not define yourself by any other yardstick. And as a precious daughter of the Most High God, it is from *that* place you should decide how to act:

Fill in the blanks from Philippians 1:27–28a (NIV translation)

"Whatever happens, _____ yourselves in a manner worthy of the Gospel of _____. Then, whether I come and see you or only hear about you in my absence, I will know that you _____ in one spirit, contending as one man for the faith of the gospel without being _____ in any way by those who _____ you.

3. *Satan will attack through both the* unyielded *and the* unprotected *areas of our lives.*

For the "unprotected" areas you may have in your life, see yesterday's lesson about where your wall might be crumbling, leaving you vulnerable. There is an app for that.

Let's talk about the "unyielded" areas – where you are holding out on God and you know it. This is commonly called a "stronghold", and in this case, it describes an action or pattern of behavior, or a *knot-filled* way of thinking that is a willful sin. We persist in it.

> *Let not sin therefore rule as king in your mortal (short-lived, perishable) bodies, to make you yield to its cravings and be subject to its lusts and evil passions. Do not continue offering or yielding your bodily members to sin as instruments (tools) of wickedness. But offer and yield yourselves to God as though you have been raised from the dead to life, and your bodily members to God, presenting them as implements of righteousness. Romans 6:12–13 (Amplified Bible translation)*

Don't we prefer the word "cravings" to the words "lusts" and "evil passions"? Cravings sound a little innocent, more respectable in polite society, more explainable. They're not. They come from the same root, and because of their "innocent" reputation, may be more insidious because we think they don't matter much, and so we let them slide, unattended. We kind of scoot them under the rug with our feet.

Last summer I had my two favorite people over: my little niece and five-year-old nephew. They love Aunt Heather's house! After they left from a long weekend with us, I began to clean up on Monday, and I kept smelling something – and it was pretty awful. I passed the mudroom and sniffed like a bloodhound, trying to find the smell, the evidence of something. It smelled like puke. I finally followed my snout to the corner of the rug and lifted the corner, and there it was. Puke.

"'Well,' said my nephew, 'I ate too much candy and pizza and my tummy got hurt on the corner of the table, and I didn't want anyone to know so I hid it under the rug.'

"Secrets smell! Best to throw open the windows, air them out, clean them up, and deal with them."

Do you have cravings you are not yielding to the lordship of Jesus Christ?

What are you hiding under the rug? Eventually it will stink!

Confess it, and turn it over to the lordship of Jesus. Strip the enemy of this weapon he uses to bludgeon you.

1 Peter 5:7 states that we should turn over, or cast, "all our anxieties on Him, because He cares for us."

Sometimes when we are at the end of our ropes, we feel ourselves slipping. Our grips begin to weaken, and we are almost to the end when our hands find the knot. Something to hold onto.

Not all knots are bad. Knots can also mean security – safety – that we are held fast and won't drift off.

Knots: So good. Grab hold of a promise to match your pain and hold on tight:

"When I said, 'My foot is slipping,' Your love, O Lord, supported me. When anxiety was great within me, Your consolation brought joy to my soul." Psalm 94:18–19

Let Him pull you in.

"I have loved you with an everlasting love; I have drawn you with loving kindness." Jeremiah 31:3

SESSION FOUR: RUNNER'S ROADBLOCKS

Day Four "Runner's Toe"

Therefore, *if anyone is in Christ, he is a new creation; the old has gone, the new has come!* *(2 Corinthians 5:17)*

"Runner's Toe" is also called "black toenail" because of its ugly appearance. It is common among runners, and first noticed as some bleeding under the toenail. It is not a serious injury, but it does hurt! And it can prevent a runner from participating, and take days, weeks, or months to heal. The healing comes when the blood under the toe works its way out – and *while the healing takes place, the area under the toenail is the perfect environment for infection.*

I'll bet that with that last sentence, you can figure out where we're going with this spiritually.

But wait, there's more …

The Runner's Toe is caused by *repeated pressure downward – constant friction –* when the foot is most vulnerable (swelling during hot weather). If enough damage has occurred, *the toenail can fall off.*

The pressures of life, the damages of our sin, the irritation of the journey can cause parts of us to turn black and fall off.

Today's lesson is about forgiveness and freedom.

I am going to share a very personal story (mentioned in Session One) that comes from a place of great pain in my past: a blackness in me that took years of believing in God and His Word, and the covering of the forgiveness of Christ, before I healed. Heal, I did. Because do you know what happens after the infection is gone and the black toenail falls off? A new nail is born. The new toenail is clean and healthy and beautiful!

... to bestow on them a crown of beauty instead of ashes, *the oil of gladness instead of mourning, and a* garment of praise instead of a spirit of despair. *They will be called oaks of righteousness, a planting of the Lord for the display of His splendor. They will rebuild the ancient ruins and* restore the places long devastated; *they will renew the ruined cities that have been devastated for generations ... Instead of their shame, my people will receive a double portion, and instead of disgrace they will rejoice in their inheritance; and so they will inherit a double portion in their land, and* everlasting joy will be theirs. *(Isaiah 61:3–4, 7) (Emphasis added)*

Here are my blackened ashes:

I was 22 years old when I made the decision to have two abortions within six months of each other. And the pregnancies had resulted from two different partners. It is now hard for me to even comprehend, but I was young, foolish, careless, and promiscuous, and had no relationship with God. I continued to party – "It was no big deal!" I thought. I had no healthy sense of who I was, I had little confidence in what I had to offer, my heart was cold, and I had no moral conscience. My parents were going through a divorce after 27 years of marriage, so the last thing they needed to hear was that their college-student daughter was pregnant. And then pregnant again. I simply wanted it done and over with and to get on with my life: a life that had no sense of purpose or direction.

It wasn't until five years later, when I was married and pregnant again, that the full weight of what I had done began to sink in. I started feeling things I did not want to feel. Denial wasn't working for me anymore. What I had kept a dark secret was surfacing. My desire to "feel" good and "forget" caught up with me, and in the end I was miserable and empty."

Here are three ways we try to deny our ashes:

1. *Deny* the impact.

   We tend to convince ourselves it doesn't matter because "I was young" or "the past is in the past." We rationalize the details so that we don't feel pain.

   What event or person in your past still follows you around?

2. *Deny* the act.

   In my case, I convinced myself that abortion was legal, after all, and that it was my right to perform the action.

   What rationalizations have you used to erase the memory?

3. *Deny* the facts.

   We make the argument and convince ourselves of it from a different perspective. I kept saying that it was only a blob of tissue and not a baby yet.

   How have you denied the facts in your situation? Do you blame others for your actions or words so that you don't find yourself guilty?

Here is His Beauty:

A few years after my son was born, I was born again! When I crossed over the line of faith, I remember "going forward" in my first church home and laying this burden on the altar. I asked God to forgive me and help anchor my fragile soul. I knew I was forgiven based on the promises of scripture, but my heart yet struggled emotionally: I would squirm at the site of anti-abortion bumper stickers, and my children's birthday celebrations would trigger deep guilt. I would look at my amazing husband, whom I adored, and live with fear and shame that he did not know what was causing me so much inner turmoil.

It was the devoted study of God's Word that began to move me in the direction of true and thorough healing. God's Spirit helped me one piece at a time. At times I would just sit and soak in a biblical phrase or promise, and something in me would start to heal, release, and blossom. I was getting better from the inside out ... my marriage was made stronger in Truth ... God began to call me to ministry with women and use my story to reach out to others who had never thought they'd hear this kind of testimony in church.

Here are some steps toward receiving your crown of beauty!

Remember *the character of God. Focus on Him.* Your Heavenly Father is *strong* and *good*! Look up the following scripture passages and say them out loud: John 14: 25–27, Psalm 16:1–2, Psalm 107:14–15.

Remember *the act and bring it out of the dark.*

Look up Hebrews 4:13 and write it below.

Ask *for forgiveness from the Father who* loves *you.*

Psalm 25:11
1 John 1:9

Come before Him and lay it all out there. He already knows. Agree with Him. Wait on Him. Receive Him.

Accept God's forgiveness.

Psalm 32:1–2
Isaiah 43:25
Psalm 103:12

Feelings are unreliable, and will sway with any breeze. *Know* that you are forgiven, and holler any of the above verses when you feel yourself slipping. Reminding yourself of truth *will* change your heart.

Release *the memory to God.* This was crucial for me in the healing over my abortions. By pulling up the memories, I would send myself back there, with the sights and sounds and emotions of the procedure room. When we intentionally release the memory to the care of God, the Holy Spirit begins to fill in the cracks and reshape how we approach what happened. Our stories will take on a new meaning in Christ, for the glory of the kingdom of God (1 John 2:27).

The final step is the refreshment of Living Water (Isaiah 43:18–19). See this week's *Extra Lap* for some of that fresh water to make streams in your wasteland!

Friends, I am grateful for the company on this patch of road. Take a deep breath and know that Christ is the balm for your deep wounds. Let your mind rest in these basic steps that healed my weary soul. In the Isaiah 61 passage on the first page of today's work, the prophet talks about restoring the ruins, giving them new life and new purpose. If you are allowing a secret to fester, I want you to take that big ruin and Run it out with the big I AM!

I'd like you to see something that might help cement this lesson into your memory. If you take the "I" out of "ruin," what you have left is "run." Don't you suppose that when we get rid of our "I" – which is our focus on our own selves – and instead Run with Christ Jesus, the "ruin" is redeemed into a whole new word? A whole new possibility? A whole new hope and a future?

SESSION FOUR: RUNNER'S ROADBLOCKS

Day Five Personal Running Log

Pace yourself

Review the week's work: the scripture you have covered, the writings on the lines and in the margins. What would you ask God for this day? What did you not quite get this week? How can you serve Him more? Who and what should you be praying for?

P Pray.
A Ask for God's vision for your life.
C Communicate back to God.
E Enter His Race for your life.

Run free in the space below: _____

Recovery questions

   ***What main thing did the study push me to *do*, *be*, or *feel* as a result of the material?

***What did God say to me through this week?

***How is my Run measuring up to these words? What action(s) will I take to bring my life in line with the words/messages received this week?

My challenge

With what truth do I need to study and Train harder?

BLISTER:

"Ouch and Pinch": Jot down those moments this week that caused pain.

BLISS:

"Praise You and Thank You": Jot down your praises.

Team Spirit/Sharing Challenge: Think of someone you know who is limping right now. _____

Pray for them.
Look for an opportunity to share with them what you have learned this week.

Theme verse:

Do you not know that in a race all the runners run, but only one gets the prize? Run in such a way as to get the prize. Everyone who competes in the games goes into strict training. They do it to get a crown that will not last; but we do it to get a crown that will last forever. Therefore, I do not run like a man running aimlessly; I do not fight like a man beating the air. No, I beat my body and make it my slave so that after I have preached to others, I myself will not be disqualified for the prize. (1 Corinthians 9: 24–27)

Write out the verses in the space below.

Pray the verses back to God, making them personal.

When you've memorized them, share the verses by speaking them out loud to your small group! Great job!

The Extra Lap

Many times our circumstances leave us feeling tired, dry, scorched, and parched.
How about a refreshing drink of Water?

Over the years as I would speak to women, I would use the following illustration:

I would challenge a volunteer to eat seven to nine Saltine crackers.

Can you imagine her face after about cracker number nine? There is a gummy texture
in her mouth, as the salt saps the moisture right out of it. Her mouth is uncomfortably
dry, and she's a little nervous to cough and a little afraid to try and swallow,
because she might choke. She looks at me as though I am an instrument of torture.

Now, imagine her relief when I hand her a glass of water: immediate refreshment!

The saltine crackers are the circumstances in our lives that leave us
depleted and dehydrated and our gaits all gummy.

I remember miles 20–24 in my very first marathon. My legs were
stiff and sore and hard, and I was Just. Plain. Tired. *My mouth*
was dry as cotton and all I could taste was the salt from my sweat
as it ran down my face. I craved water, water, WATER!

Here are a few facts about the wisdom of staying hydrated. Staying well hydrated throughout the day benefits you in ways beyond your running. First thing in the morning, a drink of water helps wake up your internal organs and get your system moving. A drink of water keeps your throat lubricated so that you can speak without rasping and let drain what needs to drain. Water keeps you alert, energized. Water keeps your skin from flaking and nails from breaking. Water can prevent muscle spasms, kidney and bladder infections, and the late-afternoon dull headache.

During my training runs leading up to this marathon, I would go out ahead of time and hide water along my path. That way, as I would start to tire and thirst, I could visualize the next stop where I knew there would be a bottle of water waiting for me. Knowing the water was just ahead would keep me going. And once I had drunk the water, I would be refueled and ready to finish.

We are now going to cross into Living Water. Read *John 4:1–26.*

Why did the woman need water? What may her daily tasks have been that required water?

_____

Water cleanses, nourishes, and dissolves.

The water in this context came from "Jacob's Well", which today is 100 feet deep. (It was probably deeper in Jesus' time.) Water was drawn with a rope and a bucket. The wells were situated outside of towns, and they became the local gathering places. Often men would gather for refreshment and discussion in order to make decisions regarding the community. Most women would gather separately in the early-morning hours or late evening. Women also would visit and chat during these hours before the day grew hot. But this Samaritan woman came to the well during the hottest time of day so that no one would see her. She had a reputation, and was hiding.

In what ways do you hide?

_____

The Samaritan woman thought she'd figured out how to hide.
Jesus found her. Living Water cleanses, nourishes, and dissolves.

155

John 4:13–14 says, "Jesus answered, 'Everyone who drinks this water will be thirsty again, but whoever drinks the water I give them will never thirst. Indeed, the water I give them will become in them a spring of water welling up to eternal life.'"

What do the words "…the water I give them will become in them a spring of water welling up to eternal life" mean to you? _____

Jesus' words are reminiscent of Isaiah 12:3. Look it up and write it below: _____

Jesus will meet you at the well along the path of your Run. He is waiting at every stop to quench your thirst with His Truth.

Look up the following scripture passages and jot down the main theme of each in the space provided: _____

Isaiah 55:1

Revelation 22:17

Jeremiah 2:13

Psalm 42:1–2

The last eight words of that last passage, Psalm 42, are, "When can I go and meet with God?" That sounds an awful lot like planned hydration.

In what specific ways can you keep yourself spiritually hydrated throughout the day? Throughout your Run?

The Samaritan woman's conversation with the Lord is His longest one-on-one chat recorded in Scripture. And it was a scandalous one by the laws of the day:

- Jews weren't supposed to speak to Samaritans (a long-standing generational tradition of bigotry and resentment).
- Men weren't permitted to address women without their husbands present.
- Rabbis had no business speaking with promiscuous women.

Jesus broke the man-made rules to honor the Kingdom purposes. He says in John 4:10, "...If you knew the gift of God ..."
If you only knew.
Can you hear Him saying that to you today?
"I know the injury is hard ... I know the path is long ... I see the fresh wound ... I know you are so very, very tired and thirsty. *But,* all of My consolation, strength, and healing is available to you: please just drink. Don't you know that the biggest work is done in the hardest miles? Please just drink. If you could see this as I see this − how the end result is worth every wince; please, just drink. I am right here. Closer than your next breath."

- Do you have a fresh wound?
- Do you have a healing wound?
- Do you have a wound that has scarred over?
- Do you have a wound that has been healed?

Drink deeply. Savor the quench of His Spirit. Amen.

SESSION FIVE

All In

1 CORINTHIANS 9: 24–27

Do you not know that in a race all the runners run, but only one
gets the prize? Run in such a way as to get the prize. Everyone
who competes in the games goes into strict training. They do
it to get a crown that will not last; but we do it to get a crown
that will last forever. Therefore, I do not run like a man running
aimlessly; I do not fight like a man beating the air. No, I beat
my body and make it my slave so that after I have preached
to others, I myself will not be disqualified for the prize.

SESSION FIVE: LECTURE NOTES

SESSION FIVE: ALL IN

The Warm-up

Following Jesus is clearly more than a leisurely stroll in the park. When you become His follower, you are in the *Race*. Period. So the question isn't, *"Will* I Run?" The question is, *"How* will I Run?"

In today's culture, it is easy to make accommodations. Being "spiritual" is very *now*. Since God planted eternity in our hearts, most humans recognize something of value in tapping into their spiritual nature. The problem is that there are so many spiritually counterfeit choices in the buffet line! So spiritual shoppers begin cherry-picking from various belief systems, and humans design their own religions, their own idols, just as humans have done since the beginning of time.

"Therefore, I do not run like someone running aimlessly."

Are believers any better off? We are certainly called to be. There are so many hazy-fuzzy-feel-good teachers out there that lure us into thinking that once we "accept Christ," there is nothing more to do but ... wait to die? And until then, coast? "Yeah, I'm a Christian, but I'm not going to knock myself out over it ..."

The stakes are infinitely higher than that.

"Everyone who competes in the games goes into strict training. They do it to get a crown that will not last, but we do it to get a crown that will last forever."

What you do with your life – the way you Run your Race and Fight the Fight – will make the difference between sharing in the promises of the gospel and *being disqualified.* Paul warned the Corinthians to examine themselves to see whether they were in the faith: "Do you not realize that Christ Jesus is in you – unless, of course, you fail the test?" (2 Corinthians 13:5) To be disqualified means that Christ is not in you. The Race has been Run in vain.

This week's goal is to fully understand Paul's admonishment to Run hard for the *gold*, to win the *prize* ... to *win*. That means strict Training: all-in, full-energy,

161

day-by-day and moment-by-moment, laser-like focus on the higher things of God. We are going to give everything to that pursuit.

All in: surrendering all of you to all of Him. God calls us to consecrate ourselves to Him. Look what Joshua 3:5 proclaims: *Consecrate yourselves, for tomorrow the Lord will do amazing things among you.* "Consecrate" means to set apart and dedicate to a higher purpose. That's *our part* of the Race.

Doing amazing things in the midst? That's *God's part.*

Our struggle is that we often try to separate the two. We want the "amazing-things" results from God without the consecration on our end. Or we try to consecrate ourselves, but it's really, really hard to do so because we are trying to consecrate without God.

Now is the time to see clearly that the combination that God set up – our full dedication *with* His power and glory – makes for the strongest possible outcome: *dangerous Runners.* You may be just one decision away from being a totally different Runner aiming at an unexpected and amazing finish. Are you all in?

Love from the center who you are; don't fake it.
Run for dear life from evil; hold on for dear life to good.
Be good friends who love deeply; practice playing second fiddle.

Don't burn out; keep yourselves fueled and aflame.
Be alert servants of the Master, cheerfully expectant.
Don't quit in hard times; pray all the harder.
(Romans 12:9–13, The Message)

Prayer:

God, you have me!
I am all Yours and thank You for the marked Race You prepared in advance for me to Run.
Please pour a desire into me to surrender all that I am to You, and so I experience a life of abundance, satisfaction, and delight in my every tomorrow.
I desire to Run dangerously *in Your anointing.*
Psalm 23:5 says that You anoint my head with oil and my cup runs over.
Amen!

SESSION FIVE: ALL IN

Day One "Take Aim"

For most long-distance runners, the first couple of miles are always the toughest. I personally have to tell myself that I cannot base my future goal on what I am experiencing thus far! If I were to base my entire run on the first two miles, I would quit!

"Forward motion toward the destination is progress."

In order to make it through those cumbersome, heavy-footed early miles, runners need to fix their eyes and take *aim* for the "forward and onward." You see, if we run with our heads down, looking at the gray, boring pavement, we tend to moan about the miles, and then what rises up is a mental block between us and our destiny/destination. We get consumed with placing one plodding foot in front of the other, and the familiar rhythm lulls us into the habit of apathy and, "Oh, well ..." (said in your best Eeyore voice).

We are to look straight ahead and fix our eyes on what lies before us, not what is going on beneath our feet! How do we do this? In order to lift our heads up and raise our perspective out of the underneath and into the future-above-and-beyond, we need to Run this life with *binocular vision.*

I love my binoculars at our family lake house. Many times I cannot see what is going on across the lake, but when I put those binoculars to my eyes it takes my line of sight right into the boats scattered across the lake. You bet I love my binoculars when my teens have the pontoon out, trolling the waters! The binoculars bring what is in the far distance close so that I can see it with clarity and focus.

God desires to give us His powerful binocular vision. God loves to delight His children by zooming in on pieces of our Races *ahead* in order to help us stay motivated in the *present*.

> *Look straight ahead, and fix your eyes on what lies before you. Mark out a straight path for your feet; stay on the safe path. (Proverbs 4:25–26) (New Living Translation)*

Do you know what you are aiming at? Do you have a distinct theory of your life's purpose that you can put into half a dozen words? Jot below.

If you have been a Christian for any length of time, you probably wrote, "Do God's will."

That is a correct answer, but often a hazy one because we struggle to make out the contours of what that looks like – how it plays out in the practical dailiness of our lives.

What are you aiming for? Some possible targets:

+ Your relationship with Jesus?
+ Your marriage?
+ Your attitude?
+ Your dreams, according to your talents and gifts?
+ Your parenting?
+ Living free of a stronghold?
+ Physical care of yourself?
+ Financial freedom?
+ Your illness?
+ Your fear or failure?

So let's get out our binoculars and take aim.
> *We're going to zoom in for a bit, and then aim straight for the bulls-eye.*

Zooming in:

Look up Genesis 49:1 and write it below.

It is truly a wake-up call to contemplate both our present and future lives. In the verses of this chapter, Jacob gives his last words to his 12 sons. All of them, regardless of their faithfulness, have futures with God and are blessed by God, because through them the 12 tribes of Israel will be founded. *But* only the *faithful* sons will have inheritance in the land.

Whoa. Let that sink in for a moment.

The lesson is clear: You and everyone you know will meet God. And God can and will work through whomever He chooses to accomplish His purposes.

But only the faithful will enjoy the inheritance.

The actions of believers determine their future blessings. And the choices believers make today will affect their descendants for generations to come.

Are you Running in such a way that has you aiming for that day to come? What specific choices are you making that are consistent with that Aim in your life? And in which areas could you use some holy help?

How is your Run setting a faithful example to those Running behind you? Think about how your loved ones would put together a one-sentence wrap-up of your life. What would they say?

Aiming straight for the bulls-eye:

When I think of taking aim, I think of growing up at the race track with my maternal grandparents. We lived at the race track and I was trained at a young age to pay attention to the traits that would determine which horse would win and why. We had about 10 racing horses, and one of them was named after me: "Tidy Heather." And we won some races!

Tidy Heather (horse), young Heather, and Heather's grandmother

Look up Psalm 32:8–9 and write it below.

The bit and bridle are already in your mouth, and it's pulled to one side or the other, which determines the direction of your trot. Tug to the right, and you are ruled by what you *know and believe*. Tug to the left, and you are ruled by what you *feel*.

Who has the reins?

Plenty of us buck at the thought of a bridle. We veer wildly between raging emotions and what we think we know, and although we may kick up a lot of dust, we never really end up near the winning circle. It is completely possible to do life without any sense of direction or completion. Billions of people do this every day. You see, God does not force us to accept His hold on the reins.

But if we accept the authority of the One in the saddle, God's Spirit will guide us surely, steadily forward, gently and sometimes in increments – a little adjustment here, a little adjustment there – so that we finish well.

As we wrap up today, we're going to use God's Word to get comfortable within the loving bridle He would have us wear. Use the verses below, and "listen" for the pressure points of the bridle to turn one way or another. Write out not only the verse, but also your spirit's immediate response to it. When we learn to interact with Scripture in this way, we find there is much God wants to say! And He wants to say something specific and unique to you and you alone. Don't miss it.

Remember your identity:

Look up Colossians 3:1 and write it below. _____

_____

What was your spirit's response to the passage? _____

Renew your thoughts:

Look up Colossians 3:2 and write it below. _____

_____

What was your spirit's response? _____

Release the old, replace with God's new:

Read Colossians 3:5–14.

How was your spirit stirred by these words? _____

Be ruled by Christ:

Read Colossians 3:15–17, and write out your gratitude for His reins holding you. How are the pressure points of the bridle and reins protecting you? Saving you? Restoring you? Prodding you forward on a straight path? _____

Psalm 32:9 says: "Do not be like the horse or like the mule, which have no understanding but must be controlled by bit and bridle or they will not come to you."

If *the horse* is one that runs ahead and is impatient …

If *the mule* is stubborn and won't move …

Would you consider yourself more like the horse or the mule? *Both* need the harness of the Holy Spirit. *Allow Christ to bring you under His control!*

SESSION FIVE: ALL IN

Day Two "Mind over Matter"

There is an old adage about what it takes to run: "Running is 90% mental and 10% physical."

In yesterday's work, and with our binoculars lifted to the horizon, we zeroed in on where to place our sights. Today, we are addressing how to change our minds. Um ... wait ... let's set aside the woman's prerogative about changing her mind and do this biblically instead: allowing God's Spirit to change and shape and actually rewire *how we think*.

From his book *A Shepherd's Look at Psalm 23*, Phillip Kellar offers us a unique perspective of our lives as sheep under the protection and care of our Shepherd. In the commentary on "Thou anointest my head with oil," Kellar talks about the actual practice of a shepherd with a flock of sheep. The flock is herded from the homestead (where everything is so carefully supplied by their owner) out to the green pastures, along the still waters, up through the mountain valleys, and to the high ground. Here, it would appear that the sheep are in a great setting in the high meadows: there are clear, running springs, the grass is fresh and tender, they are resting and feeding, and they are in close proximity to the shepherd. All seems well.

Until a fly appears.

Sheep are especially troubled by the nose fly. These little flies buzz about the sheep's head, attempting to deposit their eggs on the damp mucous membranes of the sheep's nose. If the flies are successful, the eggs will hatch in the next few days to form small, slender, worm-like larvae. These larvae work their way up the nasal passages, into the sheep's head. They burrow into the flesh and there set up an intense irritation accompanied by severe inflammation.

Grossed out yet?

For relief, sheep deliberately beat their heads against trees, rocks, posts, or brush. In extreme cases of intense infestation, a sheep may even kill itself.

Because of all this, nose flies hover around the flock. Some of the sheep become frantic with fear, sending the whole flock into panic. To avoid this, at the first sign of nose flies, the shepherd applies an ointment – an antidote – to the sheep's heads for protection. Immediately, the sheep starts to feed quietly again, and soon lies down in peaceful contentment.

For the buzzing around and within our own heads …
>   *… and for the infestation of lies that may have burrowed into our thinking many years ago …*
>   *… may we allow the Shepherd to anoint our heads, and our minds, with His oil,*
>> *which is both protective and curative.*

Before we get into our Bible lesson for today, here is a Strength Training Tip that can be useful to help shake off the "nose flies" you may encounter:

When the buzzing comes, pause and ask the Holy Spirit to
help you sort out exactly what is nipping at you:
"What do I believe to be true in this situation?"
There is something you are buying into, whether true or
not, and it is troubling you. Identify it. State it.

Now picture yourself sitting before Jesus. He has lifted and cupped your
face, and He is smiling into your eyes. He pours out some cleansing
and soothing oil into His scarred hands, and then pours the oil onto
your head and rubs it gently into those places that are tense.
Trust His touch.
Ask for His truth.
Rest, and graze on His Word as long as
you need in order to see the Truth in the situation.

Reframe the situation, this time with what you know to be true,
and state it with grace and mercy and *thanksgiving.*

Thank your Shepherd for the rescue, the balm, and the safe
pasture. And when the flies try again? (They will.)
Remember that you have already dealt with this, and
His oil and His touch are protective.

Repeat as necessary. Now, on to our Bible lesson:

Read John 5:1–9 and answer the following questions:

What was the name of the gate in Jerusalem where Jesus went for this healing miracle? _____

Who was the perfect Passover Lamb sacrificed for us? _____

What was the name of the pool of water? (It likely translates to "house of mercy".)

For how many years had the sick man been by the gate? _____

In those 38 years, among the large number of sick, the lame man had never been the first in line. You see, the tradition of this particular pool of water was that it was stagnant until an "angel" gave it a stir, which only happened now and then. And then only the first person in the water *after* the waters were stirred was healed. Supposedly. And this is where we come to a screeching halt.

Because we need to learn a little something about supernatural deception.

The account of an "angel" was attributed to superstition at the time, and references to the "angel" were not included in some early texts. Most likely, official Judaism of the time did not approve of the story. Also, a key point here is that in the John account, the appearance is referred to as an "angel," notably *not* an "angel of the Lord."

There are two kinds of angels (Revelation 12:7–9, 2 Corinthians 11:14), just as there are two kinds of prophets. (In Matthew 7:15 Jesus warns us to beware of *false* prophets). When the Bible mentions "angels" or "prophets," we need not conclude that they are agents of Almighty God. They might be agents of our enemy, Satan.

Here is where we can apply some shoe-leather to the road:

Analyze the situation about the fabled healing water of Bethesda. Before you read about supernatural deception, what did you believe about the setting of the story?
Now, let everything you know about Jesus factor into this.

- Does a stagnant pool have living water or dead water? Can dead water heal?
- Who offers Living Water?
- "Only the first one in line gets mercy." Is this how God works? Would God send an "angel" to oversee this lucky dip in dead water in which only the strongest (the one up front) stands a chance?

So this well-attended deception doesn't stack up against the Word of God or the character of God.

We now know what the Truth is: just because an event or belief system is well attended and abuzz does not make it *true*. So, what can the Holy Spirit teach us in this?

- Am I hanging around a dead pool because I'm just so desperate for the possibility of relief?
- Are there trends in our culture today in which "spirituality" is disguised as light or enlightenment, but "spirituality" is actually false, deceptive, and poisonous to our walks with Christ?
- How much does my heart break for the crowds who wait on false gods, false hope, false healing?

Jesus as Healer, Redeemer, Restorer … is true. Let's move on to the Real Deal.

We all can find ourselves paralyzed by our personal pools at times. We are unable to do a thing about it, it seems. We have those stupid nose flies buzzing around our minds: old resentment, old shame, past failures, burdens, abuses, lies about who we are and who God is. Why can't we turn off our minds? We need help to move. We desire to have even the energy to stand, let alone hope. Can our limbs even function anymore? We're here in the back of the room … does He even see us crouching here? Saying the same thing over and over again and never getting close? Will He really leave the flock to come search for me, the straggling one? Am I even worth that disruption to the schedule? Maybe I'll just hide some more.

Here comes our Savior!

> *Then Jesus said to him, "Get up! Pick up your mat and walk." At once the man was cured; he picked up his mat and walked. (John 5:8–9)*

Rise:

If Jesus says get up, we are to get up. We are finally able to do so because He said it. And we are to obey and stand to our feet and get ready to go. Yes, sometimes it means to *mentally stand up* with what the Word of God says.

- Do not make any provision to go back.
- What bridges do you need to burn?
- What do you need to cut off and move away from?

Pick up your mat:

Reject that which makes you sick and that which confined you to that lethargy. Extinguish any guilt that chirps at you: by grace you are saved! As long as your eyes are fixed on Him, you will not be needing that crutch-mat anymore!

What would Jesus have you pick up and discard today? What are you clinging to so tightly because it's all you've known for 38 years? What are you hanging onto more tightly than your faith?

And walk. Or run. Or jump and shout and kick your heels up in the air!

Do not expect to be carried if Jesus gives you the *power* to Rise and Run! Keep going!

Oh, Sister.

The Living Water, the True Healer, the Lord Jesus Christ is able to do so much more than we can imagine. In no fewer than 11 instances in the Gospels, Jesus heals people who are blind and restores their sight. Interpreting this figuratively, we can imagine that Jesus wants to heal us and help us see God's world more clearly through the eyes of faith.

So let us simply ask to see the world the way Christ would have us see it.

Then wait, watching carefully for Christ's response.

Who shall separate us from the love of Christ? Shall trouble or hardship or persecution or famine or nakedness or danger or sword? As it is written:

For your sake we face death all day long; we are considered as sheep to be slaughtered.

No, in all these things we are more than conquerors through him who loved us. For I am convinced that neither death nor life, neither angels nor demons, neither the present nor the future, nor any powers, neither height nor depth, nor anything else in all creation, will be able to separate us from the love of God that is in Christ Jesus our Lord. (Romans 8:35–39)

SESSION FIVE: ALL IN

Day Three "Strict Training"

In today's focus, we will pull from Paul's words in 1 Timothy 4:8:

For physical training is of some value, but godliness has value for all things, holding promise for both the present life and the life to come.

In this brief passage, Paul contrasts physical training (beneficial) with spiritual Training (eternal). Likewise, we will draw parallels between the two, and how that can play out in your daily life: muscle doesn't build in one day, and godliness doesn't form overnight.

Consistency is one of the most important factors in both physical training and spiritual Training: You can't put a week's worth into one day. (Oh, you can try − and pay for it the next morning when you crawl out of bed!) Conditioning grows steadily and gradually and without too much pain if you commit four days a week to training − and keep at it, week after week. Likewise, you cannot seek and serve God in spurts and expect to have great success!

This is my number-one personal weakness: discipline, both physically and spiritually. I am currently in training and place very heavy goals in front of me to accomplish more. Honestly, this is *so* hard for me! I do not get excited over my daily runs. In fact, I can even work up a good dislike for the people in the gym who are just so very committed to their workouts and thrilled to be there. Give me a break! That's so not me! I have to practically beat myself up to get there … please tell me we have something in common?

As a matter of fact, I have been called lazy by significant others in my life. One morning I went to the track with my husband to work on speed drills. My least-favorite activity. Ever. We had a goal to do 400 meters, broken up into drills. The first 200 meters would be as fast as our legs would take us. The second 200 meters would be a racewalk. (400 meters is about a quarter-mile.) We did that five times, and it was hot, and I was whining on the inside, and I got lazy. And dang, if my husband didn't call me out on it!

"You are just being lazy."

My husband is my very best friend and can be my biggest pusher in circumstances he knows I find hard. I get lazy in my running – I can get lazy in not wanting to read directions on how to put a piece of unassembled furniture together! He knows about my laziness and doesn't just call me out on it, but during this particular training, he was running behind me, saying, "Come on … you can do it!" He spoke truth to me and then encouraged me in the correction the whole time.

I do not really like "encouragement" when I am hot and lazy. I would much rather just quit!

But then I remember Proverbs 13:4, which says that "the sluggard craves and gets nothing, but the desires of the diligent are fully satisfied." And Hebrews 6:12: "We do not want you to become lazy, but to imitate those who, through faith and patience, inherit what has been promised."

Well, those land in a big thud on my heart, so I pick myself up and get going again.

Even though I don't want to.

So then I get to thinking … would the reaction be the same if I spoke some Truth to a sister or brother in Christ who was being *spiritually* lazy? Some days it will be hard to Run. And the only reason we will be able to push through and get back up is because we have been in Training; we are in good, solid spiritual condition. Strong spiritual condition is a result of Training in God's Word, and not settling for merely a Sunday morning happy-hour fix.

We do not want to be spiritual sluggards, so let's be *all in* as we look at the next step, because this verse is a doozy:

"No, I strike a blow to my body and make it my slave so that after I have preached to others, I myself will not be disqualified for the prize." (1 Corinthians 9:27)

Now take a look at the Amplified version:

But [like a boxer] I buffet my body [handle it roughly, discipline it by hardships] and subdue it, for fear that after proclaiming to others the Gospel and things pertaining to it, I myself should become unfit [unable to stand the test, be unapproved and rejected as a counterfeit].

To create discipline in our lives, Paul says we must strike a blow to our bodies to beat them into submission – that our bodies are as stubborn as mules and it takes a physical act to keep us on the right path.

Me? Mulish? Suddenly, this is not sounding very appealing! Until we understand the payoff.

Let the Training begin!

STRENGTH TRAINING TIP #1: Get over yourself.

Can we get past the idea that there is a magic carpet ride to mastering discipline and achieving success?

Jesus actually preceded Paul's admonishments when He said, "Whoever wants to be my disciple must deny themselves and take up their cross and follow me." Notice how the word "discipline" is based on the word "disciple"? In our first "duh" moment, as disciples we are *expected* to exhibit discipline – it comes with the job.

When I am doing speed work at the track and running hard, and my legs feel like mashed potatoes and my lungs are collapsing, my trainer friends say, "Tell your body: I am in charge here! You do what I say! On to the finish line!"

In what area of your life do you need to take power away from your appetites and bring them under the submission of Christ? _____

STRENGTH TRAINING TIP #2: Deny yourself.

We can strike a blow to the body by withholding what it wants. Practice doing this with something relatively easy and harmless, like withholding social media for a day. (Consider yourself challenged by this!)

Deny your flesh what it thinks it wants in an effort to bring it under submission. Try this and practice it for a day or so: you are teaching your body – your appetites – what this feels like. And as you build fasting into your life, you are building up your muscles and your habit of self-discipline. Do this when it is easy, and you'll be less likely to submit to something harmful for lack of self-discipline.

What is an easy thing that you can fast from? (Remember to start small.) Do it for one day, and every time you want to lurch toward what you are fasting from, recite 1 Corinthians 9:27. Come back here tomorrow and write down what happened. _____

What I will fast from:

What I learned about myself in the 24 hours:

There are strongholds that will hound you because they have been very successful points of entry for our enemy. To combat the constant assault, Paul drew the line and would allow no sin or pull of the flesh to be gratified. I have to daily strike a blow to my own very familiar strongholds. I try to keep my Race in front of me at all times. And when I feel God's Spirit talking to me deep within when I am about to step over a line He has established for me, I ask God to immediately grab me from my stupidity! One of my life verses is Galatians

5:16–25. I read it at the beginning of the week and the beginning of the weekend. It helps me make the best decisions and keeps me alive to the Spirit's nudges.

Where is a common point of entry and accusation for the enemy in your life?

Forewarned is forearmed. Read on for how to fortify against the enemy.

STRENGTH TRAINING TIP #3: Accept that all of this will be impossible without God.

Look up Ezekiel 36:27 and write it below:

Look up Galatians 5: 24–25 and write it below:

The discipline of self-control is a fruit of the Holy Spirit; therefore, "self-control" is not ultimately controlled by the self, but by the Spirit. Yes, we are to get over ourselves and deny ourselves and act in obedience. That's our part, but the *spiritual power* in self-control happens only when we press into the promises of the Word of God through self-denial, and when we trust the Spirit of God to give us strength.

Spiritually speaking, we have to be clothed with strength in order to Run a good Race. Our "gear" is critical, and in this week's Extra Lap, we will put on the full armor of God. But to wrap up today, we are going to bend over and pick up the only offensive weapon in the full armor of God with which we can strike against Satan. The Sword of the Spirit represents the Word of God, the Bible.

> *For the word of God is alive and active. Sharper than a double-edged sword, it penetrates even to dividing the soul and spirit, joints and marrow; it judges the thoughts and attitudes of the heart. (Hebrews 4:12)*

When Jesus was tempted in the desert by Satan, He countered with the truth of Scripture, setting an example for us. Satan's tactics have not changed, so the Sword of the Spirit (the Word of God) is still our best defense, and when used to shout down the lure of the flesh, it is also our best offensive tool.

Do you have scripture verses memorized? If so, write them down below. If you don't have a favorite scripture passage memorized, but know where it is, look it up and write it above. Recite it three times in a row, several times a day. It will be memorized in no time!

_____

**Hint #1: Use the voice memo function on your smartphone and speak the verse into it. Then listen to yourself over and over. It works for me! My family thinks I'm a little nuts when I talk back to my own voice …*

**Hint #2: Grab the smartphone app called "verse box." It's a "box" that gathers verses for you to flip through daily. It's one of my favorites!*

Now, speak your verse out loud! *Declare* the thing. And be ready to share it with your group.

SESSION FIVE: ALL IN

Day Four "Strike 1 … 2 … 3 … Satan's Out!"

As we have thrown ourselves into full-on commitment this week, we find that we keep bumping into the enemy of our souls.

As we "Take Aim" (Day One) we set our sights on God's ways and avoid the enemy's traps. As we let the peace of Christ dwell over our minds and allow ourselves to be anointed with Truth (Day Two), we are warned of the Deceiver and that which is Counterfeit, because while cherishing the sparkling and pure Living Water, we can't help but remember the stench of the stagnant water. And as we gird up for strict Training (Day Three), we learn of the Word and how Jesus knew His scripture and used it mightily during His time of temptation from – yup – Satan.

This is the human experience: the light and the dark, the good and the evil, the life and the death.

Why does the enemy strike down marriages?
Why do our minds become battlefields?
Why do our children struggle in making the right choices in life?
Why is there sickness and suffering?
Why does tragedy exist?

In a critical moment after hours on the cross, Jesus Himself cried out: "My God, my God … *why* have you forsaken me?" (Matthew 27:46) And in that moment, Jesus identified with every human who has ever felt lonely, isolated, forsaken, and hopeless.

Why?

Our natural impulses have us looking at life from a man-centered perspective: what's in this for *me*? How is this affecting *me*? But consistently, the Bible challenges us by insisting on a God-centered perspective. God did not create the world primarily for our benefit or to give us a seamless life. God created the world for His glory and His plans, that His redemption and restoration and eternal love would be glorified forever and ever.

We can hear that and accept it, but it may not bring us to the peace and the answers we seek. And it's not supposed to. We are humans – mere humans – and we will find no satisfaction apart from a life in God. He is our peace. He is always the answer. So yes, we are to dialogue with God through our shadows and know that this side of His full glory, we simply will not understand.

But in the meantime, when the confusion hurts, God is closer than your next breath. He will never leave you, forsake you, or expect you to do battle on your own.

Let's roll up our sleeves and pick up our gear: there is a battle to be *won*!

Yes, you have been targeted:

Look up 1 Peter 5:8 and write it below.

What follows is a very intimate account from my life. It is told carefully and prayerfully, that my testimony might help someone else and bring glory to the God Who restored my marriage and my hope.

෫෮ ෬

The enemy almost destroyed my marriage.

About three years into our marriage, with one baby already born into it, my husband and I were trying to adapt to this new life, but it was difficult. We both had come into the marriage with promiscuous appetites. Marriage was starting to feel confining, and we began to fill our insecurities with the wrong things. We would each set our eyes on a different character that seemed more exciting, thrilling, and good-looking than what was at home. Neither of us was walking with God, and so we were blinded. The enemy had it really easy because we didn't put up any fight at all. We both willingly started Running in wrong directions, and each time got a little farther away.

When I was out with girlfriends, I was not acting like a married woman. And my husband was not acting like a married man. We both played with fire. And then I became pregnant with our second child.

The pregnancy prompted me to settle down, but the memories of that time mark out some of the most painful of my life: I felt ugly, rejected, betrayed, and alone. I will never forget how absent my husband was from me during that pregnancy. I hit my valley hard! And what follows is how I progressed: I went to God's Word.

In 2 Kings 3:9–20, I learned how to view God's plans from the valley. Verse 9 says that after seven days' journey, they had run out of water for the army and the animals. I had run out of energy and hope. Verse 10 tells us that the exhausted and thirsty people asked, "Has the Lord led us here to then leave us?" I was really confused as to why God would leave me stranded in a valley or dead-end marriage. Had God really left us here in the valley?

Verse 11 tells us that God's people inquired of Him. When I hit this valley, I turned to God for the very first time. And this first lesson He taught me was to dig ditches in my valley. So I started digging. I put my back into it and made a place in my heart and my life for God to fill and redeem my ditches with His living water. God fills when we have made the space to receive Him.

Satan will go after marriages because strong, faithful marriages are God's idea, and they are the best foundation for family, for society, for community. The destruction of marriage is one of the biggest sources of great pain, resentment, and lifelong animosity – in one fell swoop, an entire family can be knocked off. Proverbs 2:19 tells us how damaging sexual sin can be. Many marriages never recover from it, but by God's grace, some do.

Mine did.

My situation was healed and my marriage was recovered by the Grace of God! Now married 17 years, my husband and I run together physically, and we strive to help each other Run with God and for God in all areas of our lives.

How did we get here? With a lot of hard work, and by refusing to give the territory to Satan. We fought back.

ഏ രു

There is a time when one must Run.

Read 2 Timothy 2:22–26 and 1 Timothy 6:11.

What are we to Run *from?*

What are we to Run *to?*

There is a time when we are to pick up our arms and fight.

Strike One: The Discipline of the Word

We need to fill our minds with the promises of God. One of the best ways to safeguard your mind against the emotional attacks of the enemy is by meditating on God's Word on a regular basis. The true meaning of meditation is to roll a thought over in your mind, again and again.

Most of us meditate on our problems. We take them out, look at them, stretch them, turn them over, set them out in the middle of the counter in a pretty vase, and make ourselves sick. And when we meditate on our problems, we leave ourselves wide open to spiritual attack.

Part of the beauty of meditating on God's Word is that we switch meditating on what troubles us with meditating on God Himself through scripture. It's a one-two punch: we shed the negative focus *and* we gain the promise and the hope-filled power of God's Word!

What verse have you learned recently that has helped you in your Race? Write it below.

_____

In what specific way has this piece of God's Word worked in you?

_____

Strike Two: Direction

> *See, I am sending an angel ahead of you to guard you along the way and to bring you to the place I have prepared. (Exodus 23:20)*

God's Spirit is ever present with us to nudge and direct – and God can send angels to go before us! As we keep our focus straight ahead, we can rest in faith, believing that God knows what we need. He knows we need protection and help to get where we need to go. He has already prepared a place ahead of us, and equipped us with the protection of His angels and His Presence to accompany us on the journey.

How are you going to seek divine direction this week and keep God in your decisions? _____

Strike Three: Determination

Determination means that you fix your eyes on Christ and keep them on Him, despite detours and distractions. It also means that you determine your response and action *before* you need it. And determination means you persevere. Period.

Want a model for determination? Paul displays it perfectly in 2 Corinthians 11:24–26 as he writes about a few happenings that could have discouraged him from his mission of spreading the gospel.

Read it and weep. And then praise God for Paul's example.

What is your preparedness plan for Satan's attacks and accusations? What are you determining? _____

Regarding your stalled mission/dream/plan, are there opportunities you have not yet explored? _____

Have you tried to go through, over, under, and around the obstacle?

You're Out! Deny Satan a foothold

> *For the grace of God has appeared that offers salvation to all people. It teaches us to say "No" to ungodliness and worldly passions, and to live self-controlled, upright, and godly lives in this present age. (Titus 2:11–12)*

What are some practical ways for you to say "No" this week?

Everything works out right in the end.
If things are not working right, it isn't the end yet!
Don't let it bother you … relax and keep on going.
When we "give it to God," it doesn't necessarily mean we put everything on hold.
We continue to labor and serve others.
We continue in the work we can do.
We do "the next thing" and "the best we can with what we have right in front of us."

The Lord works through our current circumstances to manifest His will.
Giving it to God doesn't mean we become lazy and do nothing.
Instead, we should be diligent, patient, and with an eye of faith,
work in hope, knowing the end will bring the promise!

We are all in *because we know that* in all *things,*

God works for the good of those who love Him and are called to His purposes.

Are you all in?

SESSION FIVE: ALL IN

Day Five Personal Running Log

Pace yourself

Review the week's work: the scripture you have covered, the writings on the lines and in the margins. What would you ask God for this day? What did you not quite get this week? How can you serve Him more? Who and what should you be praying for?

P Pray.
A Ask for God's vision for your life.
C Communicate back to God.
E Enter His Race for your life.

Run free in the space below:

Recovery questions

***What main thing did the study push me to do, be, or feel as a result of the material?

***What did God say to me through this week?

***How is my Run measuring up to these words? What action(s) will I take to bring my life in line with the word/message received this week?

My challenge

With what truth do I need to study and Train harder?

BLISTER:

"Ouch and Pinch": Jot down those moments this week that caused pain.

BLISS:

"Praise You and Thank You": Jot down your praises.

Team Spirit/Sharing Challenge: Think of someone you know who is limping right now.

Pray for them.
Look for an opportunity to share with them what you have learned this week.

Theme verse:

Do you not know that in a race all the runners run, but only one gets the prize? Run in such a way as to get the prize. Everyone who competes in the games goes into strict training. They do it to get a crown that will not last; but we do it to get a crown that will last forever. Therefore, I do not run like a man running aimlessly; I do not fight like a man beating the air. No, I beat my body and make it my slave so that after I have preached to others, I myself will not be disqualified for the prize. (1 Corinthians 9: 24–27)

Write out the verses in the space below.

Pray the verses back to God, making them personal.

When you've memorized them, share *the verses by speaking them out loud to your small group! Great job!*

The Extra Lap

Spiritually speaking, we have to be clothed with
strength in order to Run a good Race.

Our spiritual Race gear is critical!

God has provided the wardrobe, and it is there waiting for us.

Guess who is in charge of putting it on?

Before you pull even one item of clothing off its hanger and try it on, read Ephesians 6:10–18.
(For seasoned Christians used to going into this particular closet, you will be
very familiar with this passage and the armor of God. Read it again anyway.)

There are six items of Race Gear we will be looking at in this week's Extra
Lap: the Belt of Truth, The Breastplate of Righteousness, the Gospel of Peace
fitted on our feet, the Shield of Faith, the Helmet of Salvation, and the Sword
of the Spirit.

The book of Ephesians is a letter from the apostle Paul to the Church at
Ephesus. Paul had been living and preaching at Ephesus for a few years, and
these Christians were close to his heart. His intent in writing was to encourage
and strengthen their faith.

One of the lessons Paul teaches in Ephesians is that Christians are in a
spiritual war. We are soldiers of Christ and will be tried, tested, tempted, and
attacked by the enemy. The enemy is Satan and Satan's minions (demons,
spirits/"angels" of darkness). They present themselves in many disguises, but
they are the same enemy. Christians must always be on guard and prepared to
fight off that which we know to be sin. We must be wise and discerning to guard

against deception. Never forget that Satan was a beautiful angel: his deceptions can be clothed very nicely and appear quite attractive.

The entire purpose of a war is to crush and stomp on the enemy. *To kill.* That is Satan's purpose: to kill as many of us in the spirit as he can. Paul reminds us that we do not have to try and win anything! *The war is already won and Christ is already the victor!* The armor of God is God's provision for our protection and covering in this earthly life. The battle rages: *suit up*!

Belt of Truth

Another translation of Ephesians 6:14 puts it this way: "Stand therefore, having girded your waist with the belt of truth."

- What does a belt do?
- What does a girdle do? (For you young'uns, think "Spanx.")

A translation of 1 Peter 1:13 also uses the Greek word for girdle: "gird up the loins of your mind." That is, to pull in all the loose ends of our thinking; to rein in a wandering mind so that we might be ready and able to think clearly and discern wisely. It is a willful removal of those things that would otherwise confuse or slow down our reaction time in the face of evil.

What is it that you need to corral, rein in, contain with your Belt of Truth so that your britches don't fall down?

_____

Breastplate of Righteousness

In using this language, Paul was remembering that the Roman soldiers wore breastplates to protect their upper bodies from fiery, deadly darts. The armor covered the soldier's body from his neck to his thighs, but was primarily in place to protect his heart. In the same way, we need to protect our hearts in today's world.

Our lifestyle of righteous living serves the same purpose for us as the breastplate of armor. Our enemy will often take aim at our hearts. It is the seat of our emotions, our self worth, our trust. Christians are to strive to live righteously, with integrity, holiness, and purity of thoughts and actions.

Where is there a chink in your armor – your breastplate? In what ways does the enemy find your soft spot and use it to strike you down?

Feet fitted with the Gospel of Peace

Paul did not just write about the armor of God; he also wore it. At this time in his life, Paul found protection and strength in the knowledge of what God's gospel meant for him. He strapped on the Peace and shared the Good News with others! Paul's footing was sure and unshakable, and he was prepared to carry the gospel wherever God sent him. A shoeless soldier could not run very well in the middle of a battle because his bare feet would land on sticks, stones, debris, and dried up roots in the ground. Shoes allow us to step freely and gain traction in our Races.

The sandals of the Roman soldiers often had spikes to make them hold firm in the ground. Paul would have known this. Don't you love this imagery? God's Good News about Jesus Christ is our firm foundation, and with the gospel working for us, we are able to stand firm and grip hard the Foundation of the world that is sovereign over time and space. That's some sure footing right there!

Where is the ground shaky for you? Are you claiming God's firm foundation on a daily basis? Or is your foot slipping as you Run? Do you keep stepping on spiky things because you forgot to put your Running Shoes on?

Shield of Faith

Think about the shield of faith and what we learned about the breastplate of righteousness. The breastplate *will* protect our hearts and vital organs, but with the Shield strapped onto our arms and mobile, we can fend off slings and arrows before they even get close! No wonder the Bible says we should have it "above all." With the knowledge of Jesus Christ and the faith *in* Jesus Christ, we have available to us the power of Almighty God!

Look up 2 Peter 1:3-4 and write it below.
_____

That's right. Can we ever really overstate this? *God gives us everything we need.*

One last point: when the Roman soldiers would go to war, they would often interlock their shields to form a solid wall of protection and an intimidating line of offense for approaching the enemy. That's what you are doing in small groups, my friends! In prayer, in faith, in doing life together as a people called by God, you are interlocking and erecting a mighty wall of protection against the enemy. *Don't discount this!* Where two or three are gathered – interlocked in their faith – and calling on the name of Jesus? *Whoa, baby!*

Helmet of Salvation

Paul describes our salvation as a helmet. So, exactly, how is our salvation like a helmet?

What does a helmet cover and protect? (This is a rhetorical question. Of course you know this!) A helmet covers and protects the *head*.

1 Corinthians 2:16 tells us that believers "have the mind of Christ." Now let's go one step further: 2 Corinthians 10:5 explains that those who are in Christ have the divine power to "demolish arguments and every pretension that sets itself up against the knowledge of God, and take captive every thought to make it obedient to Christ."

The Helmet of Salvation protects our thoughts and minds.

O Sovereign Lord, my strong deliverer, who shields my head in the day of battle ... (Psalm 140:7)

Look up 1 Thessalonians 5:8 and write it below. _____

There is one very, very important four-letter word in this passage that is associated with the Helmet of Salvation. What is it? _____

Yes.

There will be seasons of our lives that will devastate and paralyze us, and during those times it will feel like *all we have is hope*. Jesus does not want us to bear this grief ... He already bore it on the cross.

Gladness and joy are our portion, not sorrow and sadness. Life is hard, but we have *Jesus*. Place that Helmet on your head and cover your mind in the *hope* that is released only through the power of the Holy Spirit. Receive it in faith. And if you are struggling with grabbing onto that hope and allowing it to release the toxins of pain, worry, and grief, simply ask like a child to a loving Father:

"Father, I can't even lift my hands to reach for the Helmet right now. Please, Abba. Place the Helmet over my head for me. Let your Spirit protect and cover me in the ongoing work of Your salvation in my life, and in my 'right now'. I need You desperately. I love You. I am so grateful for what You are protecting me from and the Hope you will place in my heart so that I can see past the 'right now'. Thank You, Father."

Sword of the Spirit

On Day Three of this week, you were asked to write down and memorize a verse of Scripture so that you would always have it at the ready for battle. Did you do so? Write it below *from memory*. (Yes, this is the part where the teacher is checking for completed homework!) Then pray it. Live it.

SESSION SIX

A Winner!

1 CORINTHIANS 9: 24–27

Do you not know that in a race all the runners run, but only one gets the prize? Run in such a way as to get the prize. Everyone who competes in the games goes into strict training. They do it to get a crown that will not last; but we do it to get a crown that will last forever. Therefore, I do not run like a man running aimlessly; I do not fight like a man beating the air. No, I beat my body and make it my slave so that after I have preached to others, I myself will not be disqualified for the prize.

SESSION SIX: LECTURE NOTES

SESSION SIX: A WINNER!

The Warm-up

The goal of every Christian should be to Run their spiritual Race to *win* – to be a disciple worthy of obtaining *the prize.* This life is the most serious competition we will ever face in this world. The Lord has called you to Run your Race toward eternity, and you have to run through the streets of chaos this side of Heaven to get there. You won't always be able to choose your streets, but you can choose to Run toward victory and not quit. The rewards are enormous: God materially rewards us as we are faithful to His call, but He also reserves eternal rewards of honor and glory for those who Run their Races well.

The apostle Paul consistently taught this central Christian truth throughout his New Testament letters, including his letter to the believers at Corinth. When Paul talked about a "crown" or "prize," he was making a reference to the most coveted athletic prize in the Roman Empire: the stephanos, or the laurel-like wreath that was placed on the heads of champions. This is the very crown Paul refers to our theme verse. Twigs? Branches? Why spend life capital on such things when the glory of Heaven and the crown of life awaits? The reality of this future prize should explode our faith and inspire us with every step of the Race.

This is a Race worth winning – and yes, you *can* win.

Unlike with an earthbound footrace, the Prize is available to each and every believer.

Unlike in an earthbound competition, you are *not* competing against others – in fact, God's Word specifically warns us against any form of comparison among His people. And isn't this Good News? There simply will always be someone faster, stronger, or smarter than us. And that matters not one whit.

Our Race is the Run in which we strive to become the people God designed us, uniquely, to be. And to use every scrap of DNA that He frontloaded into us *for the glory and purposes of God.*

Period.

As we approach our last week of homework, keep the Win foremost in your mind. What does your Win look like? What part of how God made you ...

deliberately,

uniquely,

lovingly,

and joyously

are you not allowing Him to fully light up?

With this in mind, let's finish strong. Don't quit. For the glory of God, don't quit! This week, Run with all your might. Keep your focus on the goal of God's divine calling on your life.

SESSION SIX: A WINNER!

Day One "Hidden Treasures"

The Parable of the Hidden Treasure and the Pearl

The kingdom of heaven is like treasure hidden in a field. When a man found it, he hid it again, and then in his joy went and sold all he had and bought that field. Again, the kingdom of heaven is like a merchant looking for fine pearls. When he found one of great value, he went away and sold everything he had and bought it. (Matthew 13:44–45)

In today's lesson, we will break down this scripture passage and start digging in our fields for the treasure – the fine pearls. God has a divine purpose for each of us, which He reveals through the Holy Spirit and His Word, so that we may experience the kingdom of heaven and His victory *while here on earth.*

Enjoying the kingdom of heaven while staggering through some of life's blows can seem like a stretch. Things break: marriages, relationships, children, families, ministries, jobs, our bodies – we can be whistling along one day, and the next day wonder how everyone else is going on as usual when We. Are. Going. Through. *This.*

To mark our victory laps when life bruises, we need to learn how to position our attitudes to receive immediately the hidden treasures available to us. The pearls hold the answers to everything. There may be many things in the field that we can dig up, but the perfect wisdom – the way to the truth and the Life – is through Jesus Christ. This brief and beautiful parable teaches that the kingdom of heaven is so valuable that the wise are willing to sacrifice anything in order to gain it.

Are you?

We have two fellas coming across a field.

The first one is "a man," the second is "a merchant." Many stumble across Jesus, and others seek Him.

The man – the stumbler

In the first story, Jesus tells us that treasure was hidden in a field and a man accidentally discovered it. He was just digging in a field, and there it was. The man was thrilled! He recognized the treasure for its value, and remained tight-lipped while he pursued it with everything he had. (Shrewd move! God appreciates shrewd behavior as long as it is ethical.) Please notice that the man wasn't *seeking* treasure – the treasure basically found him. So what was he doing there?

Back in Jesus' day, death, imprisonment, or exile could claim the owner of a field, separating the owner from his property. Often, the owner or the family would hire out the field, and the land could be plowed and cultivated. Regardless of how he'd come to be there, the man accidentally dug up the treasure and responded with joy, action, and perseverance. In a modern application, this might be someone who "believes" in "a God," but doesn't really do anything about it, and then *wham!* He face-plants into the reality of Jesus, recognizes what is required, and is all-in. He is entering the kingdom of heaven.

When Paul teaches us to Run in Such A Way, he is encouraging us to find Jesus in our daily Runs, be watchful of the fields on all sides, see the ground beneath our feet, be alert for His presence. *Jesus is our Treasure!* We are to see the treasure not as "coincidence," but *wham!* God breaking into our reality! And then we are to tuck the treasures away – cherish and pray over them – and go about acquiring the field.

The merchant – the seeker

This time, the finder is intentionally looking for some kind of kingdom, something to fill his needs. He doesn't stumble onto the Truth – he is hungry *for* the Truth. The merchant relentlessly pursued that which would satisfy, and his focused pursuit led to the one and only Kingdom! In a parallel for us, this may be the self-described "spiritual" person who is successful in today's marketplace, but still feels an emptiness on the inside that cannot be filled. This person may dabble in all kinds of activities and religions and belief systems, trying to find something to believe – until he finds Someone, the only One, who is worthy of belief. *Jesus is our Pearl!*

Think about a pearl for a minute.

In Jesus' day, pearls were highly prized – more valuable than gold.

Pearls form when an irritant gets into an oyster or mussel. The irritant can be a piece of shell, a food particle, bacteria, or a piece of sand. This, then, begins the protective process, and as the layers of protection surround the irritation, the pearl is formed.

All irritations in our lives are designed to become pearls. We can just choose to be irritated and cranky, and wound ourselves or others in the process. But why waste the Gift? God can use every irritation to form in us things of beauty and wisdom. Pure Treasure. When things in life don't run in the direction we planned, we should accept them as the shaping of the pearl inside us. After all, *where* you are is not nearly as important as *who* you are.

So how can we better identify the treasures and hidden pearls? This will be our focus for the remainder of today's lesson.

Pick an irritant in your life that has you digging holes around in fields looking for consolation or answers:

Look up Colossians 3:1 and write it below. _____

Where is this verse telling you to look? What kinds of things are you to pursue?

Look up Matthew 7:7. What will happen when you seek?

Look up Jeremiah 29:13 and write it below. (This is a good Pearl to tuck away in your heart.)

I have hidden your word in my heart that I might not sin against You. Psalm 119:11

Just as the merchant understood the value in a pearl and hid it in a field, we need to understand the value of God's Word and hide it in our hearts. Merchants lived their days buying, selling, evaluating, and trading pearls of great find. They were dedicated and knowledgeable about their profession and had trained eyes to see the worth of each pearl.

Have you ever met a student of the Word who was like this merchant? Who had such trained eyes that they could offer God's Word over a situation?

Do you strive to live daily to learn and find the pearls God has for you? If so, in what ways? And in what ways can you further train your pearl-finding eyes?

Do you treasure the pearls you have found? Do you memorize them? Hide them in your heart? Journal them? Trade them?

You know that current irritant you named on the previous page? Run a biblical search on pertinent words in your situation ("accusation," "patience," "fools," etc.) either online or in a concordance. Look up the applicable verse(s), write it on a card, and ponder it in your heart until you hear from God. Don't do a thing until you hear from God, and don't let your mind go anywhere else, except for to the word that is on the card.

There is at least one more prominent place in Matthew where Jesus spoke of pearls – specifically the *wasting* of pearls.

> *Do not give that which is holy (the sacred thing) to the dogs, and do not throw your pearls before hogs, lest they trample upon them with their feet and turn and tear you in pieces. (Matthew 7:6, Amplified Version)*

Who would do such a thing? Who would take that which is precious and toss it to a farm animal that has no concept of its value?

We would!

Every time we make excuses and sleep in, or get lazy and shrug off or forget the blessings and teachings and Living Words of God, we are tossing treasure to swine.

What are you throwing at pigs?
_____

Which parts of your life have you tossed aside? Where should you be digging for treasure instead?
_____

Do you struggle with valuing the good in your life? Are you surrounded by critical people?
_____

What steps can you take to reclaim your treasure today? Write it. Date it. Do it.

STRENGTH TRAINING TIP #4: *Allow God to pearlize your irritants more quickly by giving them to Him instead of your memory bank. (They're His anyway — it's just you acknowledging that and opening your clenched fist!)*

Then rise up and declare the following:
(Yes, say it out loud.)

YES, LORD. I ACCEPT IT. I SUBMIT.

HELP ME. I YIELD.

I SURRENDER.

I TRUST YOU AND THANK YOU IN JESUS' NAME.

SESSION SIX: A WINNER!

Day Two "God's Guideposts and Guardrails"

Personally, I must admit that I love the excitement behind living the Ephesians 3:20 life. "Now to Him who is able to do immeasurably more than all we ask or imagine according to His power that is at work within us ..." I truly love the journey, and the mystery, of serving Jesus. My desire is to Run like a winner – especially on days when I feel like a loser. I am so grateful that He lights up the path before me at every turn, but I have often had to learn this the hard way! Sometimes on my runs I cross over the expressway bridge on a narrow path. If I look down over the guardrail, traffic is screaming along at 75–80 miles per hour, and that's a little scary! The guardrail is not only an actual barrier preventing injury, but it is also a visual reminder that I'm safe on the path. God's Word is the protective guardrail of all time!

The most efficient path from "Point A" to "Point B" is a straight line. (You might remember this from middle school geometry.) The straight shot is the quickest and often easiest path. The line is straight. You go forward. You are done. This is what makes 50-yard dashes – or sprints of any kind – so exhilarating! Because there are no nooks or crannies to navigate, your focus is narrowed to the issue of speed. You can flat out run.

This is not the experience of our Run, however. Ours is more of a cross-country, endurance, Tough Mudder, Iron Man kind of experience: Just when you think you can see 20 yards ahead, there is a pool of water to jump over. Then there is a wall to scale and drop from. And, oh yes, watch out for the fallen limbs and the snakes. Always the snakes.

The Christian life has often been compared to a battlefield laden with landmines. We can try to make it through without getting blown to bits, *or* we can listen to the One who knows where the explosive devices are and can help us step carefully.

Guideposts: At this point in the study, a lot of the Race is in the rearview mirror. No matter our age or the length of the track, we have a *history* with God now. What have we learned? There are thousands of years' worth of instruction and wisdom transcribed in the Bible. Are we missing anything?

Guardrails: The good way forward is learning from the road you went down and staying within the areas of safe passage. Guardrails warn of dangers and mark the curves. They also alert us when a cliff is approaching. The idea is not to have the guardrail right at the edge of the cliff, but with enough distance ahead of the danger so you have time to adjust, stop, and prevent.

Forward motion: Would a game be fun to play if you never advanced from one level to the next? Isn't the excitement of a win due to anticipation of the next challenge? How dull would life be if we were victorious in one area of our lives, but then the victory didn't lead to the next challenge?

GUIDEPOSTS

Can we just do a little happy dance for God's consistent, clear, and eternal *one-way* sign? Hallelujah! From before time began, and before one "let there be light" was uttered, there was but one way to salvation, restoration, and redemption in the person of Christ Jesus. The longest quoted Old Testament passage to appear in the New Testament is from Jeremiah, chapter 31. This batch of prophetic verses reaches all the way back to Eve, through Abraham and David, and assures the future that Christ will grant believers new hearts and fellowship with Him. Talk about a guidepost.

Look up Jeremiah 31:21 and write it below.

These road markers and signposts would lead Israel back home from the captivity in Babylon and serve as reminders of the "ancient paths" they had traveled with God. As we have addressed before in this study, Israel – God's people – struggled to remember Almighty God and His ways, and were known for backsliding and lightning-fast disobedience.

We live in a day when our culture dislikes the word "sin," and breaks a sweat to even declare anything really "wrong." The pervasive culture preaches that you can be your own god and make your own rules, and do whatever you want with your body, your words, your actions. This sounds a lot like idolatry.

We come from an ancient tradition and a mighty God: we have thousands of years of recorded words and deeds and rich presence and relationship with the Living God. Of the many "ancient paths" we have touched on in this study (God's sovereignty, faithfulness, law, love, direction, beautiful language, symbolism, radiance, promise, a hope, and a future) ... what is the *very first* thing that rose up in you? (Write it below.)

Now, in your opinion, what within you is attracted to that piece of history or character of God? (Whatever you wrote down, pray on it and ask God to further nudge and satisfy you.)

One more consistent thread woven into us from 640 BC (Jeremiah's birth) stretches out to this very day: such love of His Word! Look up Jeremiah 15:16 and write it below.

GUARDRAILS

We have handled at length in this study the wisdom, the warning, the affirmations of Scripture and God's ways and law. We are all works in progress, and as long as we are breathing, we have the choice to grow and develop, and that is why we Run. All of that admonishment and counsel is important, relevant, and the only way to an abundant, meaningful life.

But for our purposes today, let's consider no guardrails at all and ponder the idea of truly unlimited growth. But in a creepy way.

There is an old German fictional character named Zarathustra who speaks of the "cripple in reverse," a figure who had an earlobe that would not stop growing. It extended from his head to the ground, and kept growing from there. Eeewwww! It is a wonderful thing in our lives that inherent in our development is the guided growth provided by God's guardrails. This guided growth allows new things to *start* growing because old things *stop* growing. It's important to understand the distinctions.

Look up Ephesians 4:14–15, read it, and answer the questions below.

1. In what ways might you still be an "infant" of the faith? (Your beliefs and opinions are determined by the persuasive person you last talked to, for example.)

2. Is there anything in your life that has unfettered, unlimited growth, and you know very well it's kind of gross looking?

3. In your life, what New Growth might be stunted because you are reluctant to pull up the roots of some old growth that needs to go?

213

FORWARD MOTION

Because who wants to stand still?
Two readings to nourish you:

"So, how'd you like your heart attack?"
     "It scared me to death, almost."
"Would you like to do it again?"
     "No!"
"Would you recommend it?"
     "Definitely not."
"Does your life mean more to you than it did before?"
     "Well, yes."
"You have always had a beautiful marriage, but now are you closer than ever?"
     "Yes."
"How about that new granddaughter?"
     "Yes. Did I show you her picture?"
"Do you have a new compassion for people – a deep understanding and sympathy?"
     "Yes."
"Do you know the Lord in a richer, deeper fellowship than you had ever realized could be possible?"
     "Yes."
"How'd you like your heart attack?"

Silence was his answer.

                    (From *Something's Going On Here* by Bob Benson)

Listen to your life. See it for the fathomless mystery it is. In the boredom and pain of it no less than in the excitement and gladness: touch, taste, smell your way to the holy and hidden heart of it because in the last analysis all moments are key moments, and life itself is grace.

                    (From *Now and Then* by Frederick Buechner)

SESSION SIX: A WINNER!

Day Three "Obtain the Prize"

George Watson was a mine worker-turned Methodist preacher in the late 1800s. The story is told of his writing a book based upon a vision he'd had. He had dreamed that he had gone to Heaven, and seen a great factory where angels were making crowns for the saints: countless crowns of all sizes, shapes, and splendor. The heavenly guide in the dream told him that when a man became a Christian, an angel was sent by the Lord to measure his head. The Christian was to carry out the work of his salvation and sharing Christ with those with whom he came into contact ... and then, once Home, he would get his crown.

Could you feel the tape measure as it encircled your head?

This is a lovely story, and today's kicking-off point for learning about the crowns awaiting the faithful. We have talked about the prize, the pearl, the presence of Jesus, the hidden treasure, and the guardrails and guideposts erected by the Holy Spirit for us – all "prizes" we get to enjoy during our brief stint on earth. Today, we lift our gaze to beyond the horizon.

> *I have fought the good fight, I have finished the Race, I have kept the faith. Now, there is in store for me the crown of righteousness, which the Lord, the righteous Judge, will award to me on that day – and not only to me, but also to all who have longed for his appearing. (2 Timothy 4:7–8)*

When Paul was writing to Timothy, he would have had the picture in his head from the athletic competitions and award ceremonies of his time. In the Olympics, the awards were given at the "Bema Seat" (named after the Greek word for "judgment"). Yes, the judges would hand out the laurel-leaf crown, but at the Bema Seat, citizens could also approach the judges for legal disputes or to level charges against someone. Paul was very familiar with this Seat and the procedure. This is the very place Paul was brought before Gallio in Acts 18:12, having been charged with persuading people to worship God in ways contrary to the law. Paul also gave a nod to the proceedings in 2 Corinthians when he talked of the "judgment seat of Christ." It is here that believers will be rewarded or suffer loss of rewards, based on their deeds and their stewardship of God-given responsibilities (Romans 14:10–12).

You see, this Seat is for believers only! Although everyone will make an account before Almighty God at the end of their life, most interpreters distinguish between this evaluation by Christ of His servants, and the "Great White Throne," where *unbelievers* will be raised for judgment (Revelation 20:4–6). As Christ followers, we *are* covered with the blood of Jesus and there is *no* condemnation. *But there is evaluation.*

It is false doctrine to believe that just because we are saved by Jesus, we can live any way we want! Will Jesus save you because you belong to Him? *Absolutely.* Will you be evaluated and rewarded, or not rewarded, based on how you Run this Race? *Absolutely!*

So let's talk about the crowns, Princesses! You *are* daughters of the King, after all.

First, our scriptural jumping-off points:

Look up 2 Corinthians 5:10 and write it below. _____

Now, please look up Revelation 22:12 and write it below. _____

God is setting up His eternal kingdom, and He will use everything that you have endured, completed, accepted, spoken, and shouted hallelujah over to eternally reward you.

The Crown of Life – James 1:12

Have you persevered under trial in your life? Have you endured temptation and remained faithful? What do you believe it means when the verse states that you have stood the test?

Do not be afraid of what you are about to suffer. I tell you, the devil will put some of you in prison to test you, and you will suffer persecution for ten days. Be faithful, even to the point of death, and I will give you the crown of life. (Revelation 2:10)

I will bestow on them a crown of beauty instead of their ashes. (Isaiah 61:37)

The Crown of Righteousness – 2 Timothy 4:7

This is a personal crown that probably translates more accurately to "the crown that *consists* of righteousness." Thus, it will go to all true believers because our final state is standing in the righteousness of Christ.

This crown is placed on the heads of those who long for Jesus and his return.

The Incorruption Crown – 1 Corinthians 9:24–27

This is sometimes also referred to as the "Imperishable Crown". The verse it is mentioned in should be a familiar one to you after all these weeks – do you have it memorized yet?

This crown will go to the disciplined – those who strived for excellence and the winning of the *eternal* reward, not the earthly victory.

In what ways have you learned to "crucify the flesh" in favor of an eternal reward?

The Crown of Rejoicing – I Thessalonians 2:19

This crown is given to those who joyously express their faith. "For what is our hope, our joy, or the *crown* in which we will glory in the presence of our Lord Jesus when he comes …"

Other translations explicitly say *"crown of rejoicing."* If you do not joyously express your faith, you will not gain this crown, to put it bluntly. Daniel 12:3 says, "Those who are wise will shine like the brightness of the heavens, and those who lead many to righteousness, like the stars forever and ever." Many scholars take this to mean, if you lead others to righteousness by expressing your faith, you will receive a crown that will shine like the "brightness of the heavens."

Do you know of Christ followers who rejoice and give glory to God, no matter what is happening in their lives? No matter the hardship or suffering? *How have their examples, their utter trust and jubilation, impacted you or helped you to know God better?*

The Crown of Glory – 1 Peter 5:4

This crown is given to those who are faithful in ministering to the world. This ministry includes evangelism (telling others about Jesus) and shepherding (seeing to the needs within the Church and beyond it). In this scripture passage, results are not measured; effort is! Seek opportunities to minister in Jesus' name. In the few verses before 1 Peter 5:4, we read what this looks like, and it is beautiful in its simplicity: *serving. Serving!* And serving with a true heart and pure motives so that we are examples to the flock.

Do you serve in a local ministry or teach the Word of God?

Do you use the gifts that God hard-wired into you to serve and care for people in your sphere of influence, to the glory of God?

A continuation of George Watson's dream:

> *A woman came and asked where her crown might be, for she had not yet been issued one, and others she knew from her church already were wearing theirs.*
> *"Oh," the angel said. "And on what basis have you a claim of a crown?"*
> *She answered, "I witnessed in my own way."*
> *The angel asked, "So tell me, what sort of witness were you in your lifetime of Christian living?"*
> *The woman explained, "I was a silent witness."*
> *"I see," said the one in bright clothing. "Then for this silent witness you shall be given an invisible crown. Here they are. You may select one. They all fit every size, and you have your choice." The angel pointed her to the glass case that appeared totally empty.*

"But I don't see any crowns in there," she stated in her perplexity. "How are others to see that I am wearing one of these?"

"Oh," replied the angel one last time. "In the same manner which they learned of Christ through what you say is recorded as your silent witness."

The angel dispensing crowns no longer talked to her, and she no longer had any questions to ask.

Mile Marker

Lidia

For as long as I can remember, I dreamed of settling down, getting married, and having children. I waited until I was 30 to marry, but when I did, I thought we would grow old together. Neither one of us had ever committed to living for Christ, although we both believed in God, so we were following our own ideas of what marriage should or should not be. In 2004 we were married, and we eventually had two boys. We were married for 10 years. When my boys were one and three, my husband said he was leaving. It was such a painful decision for him – I could not understand why he was leaving. This came at a time when I had begun questioning the emptiness in my life and the meaning. The divorce was what catapulted me into the arms of a loving Savior who I would soon realize was alive and calling me to a relationship with Him.

My husband and I lived together for six months before he moved out and the divorce became final. Two weeks after he left, I gave my heart to Christ. During that time, God was revealing Himself to me in ways I had never known existed. I had never been taught that God wanted to interact with us on a personal level. He had always seemed unreachable to me. I began going to church and the Bible was being taught there; Bible teaching was foreign to me! I started realizing that the Bible had all the answers on how life should really be lived, and so I made a decision to go through my divorce God's way. God put a woman in my life to pray and mentor me to do just that. I was going through an awakening in my life, and suddenly I saw things so differently to how I had before. I knew divorce was not God's plan, so I committed to allowing Him to change me, and as I did, it had an impact on my husband. One day he said to me …

"God looks good on you."

I had no clue at the time why he had said that. All I knew was that somehow he was seeing on the outside what I was feeling on the inside. This gave me hope that maybe he would have his own encounter with God. He had struggles in every area of his life, and it was taking a toll. Sometimes I didn't know how he was able to survive. I remember asking God to use me to save him the way God had used him to save me. I believe that prayer was answered, but not in the way I would have thought …

Through much prayer and pruning, I treated him graciously and wondered many times if God was going to restore our marriage. How I hoped to serve God together as a family – or be a testimony to how our faith had restored our marriage! For seven years I prayed for him, and for two of those years my small group joined me in that prayer.

Then, one night, in August 2011, the man I was married to – the father of my two boys – Committed suicide.

To say I was in a daze after that is not a strong enough description. I ran through every emotion known to man, and then ran through them again and again. Although I knew he was free of his torment, I could not understand how God could allow our story to end this way. This was not the plan I'd had in mind or the dream I had seen for our family. How could this happen, and why? I was shattered and shaken to my core. After I broke the news to my kids, they ran around the house trying to find a picture of him. My sister said she would run home and get the picture she'd taken of them with him on Father's Day.

Two days later, one of the ladies in my prayer group, who was an artist, called me and said, "the Lord had me paint something for you … it's on your porch." She had never seen the Father's Day picture. Her painting was of sunflowers.

Little did she know that the month before he had died, I had been obsessing over sunflowers, reading about them and learning that they lift their faces to follow the sun(light) as it progresses across the sky.

Little did I know − not until I accidentally put the painting next to the photograph − that the composition was identical:

The big flower with his arms around the little flowers.

I used the painting in the eulogy I wrote for the funeral.

When we follow the Son, we can turn from darkness to light. (John 8:12)

I also believe that God has confirmed in my heart that my ex-husband had done just that, and was now in the arms of our Savior in heaven.

When I said that my prayer had been answered, but not in the way I had thought it would be, I meant that I recognized that the prize of a restored marriage is a temporary prize, but the prize of eternal salvation is one that will truly restore my family. As I thought about 2 Corinthians 9:23–25, I realized that our prize is that we will all be together in heaven, and as I tell my sons, that is what we remain focused on to give us hope while we finish our own Races.

I can't say that while going through all this I remained in perfect trust of God. But the constant awareness that my children are looking to me to show them the way through all of this keeps me dependent on God, because I need Him to lead me through so that I can lead them through.

It has been a process.

I have wrestled, cried until my eyes swelled, and asked Him countless questions … but the thing that keeps me going is that He is faithful. When I pulled away from Him, he waited patiently for me to return. When I cried and questioned, He listened and sometimes answered through scripture verses, other people, or my thoughts. When I didn't hear an answer to my question, I was constantly reminded of Romans 8:28, that

He wants good for me to the point that He uses everything that comes my way to get it for me!

Even the bad.

So many good things have come out of this tragedy. Some of them were just between Him and me – letting me know He was near and He saw.

It has taken time to put back the trust I withdrew from Him, and it is ongoing even now, but I have come to a place where I realize that He suffers with me, and that somehow helps me realize He is on my side and that He is *for* me, not against me.

Each day, while I wait for God to finish my story, He strengthens me. Isaiah 40:31

SESSION SIX: A WINNER!

Day Four "The Finish Line"

When marathoners gather for the start of a race, they have set goals, they have prepared and trained, they have pushed through obstacles, they have positioned themselves for launch, and they await the gunshot that signals *"Go!"* Runners know the finish line is on the other side of a 3–4 hour run, and with it, all the celebration and elation over the goal accomplished!

The Boston Marathon, birthed in 1897, has more tradition than any other major marathon in America. And in 2013, the Boston Marathon saw more tragedy than any other marathon in the world. Bombs went off near the finish line, and instead of runners and spectators rejoicing and cheering, people were crying, confused, scared, dead.

The finish line had turned into a crime scene.

As we approach our final week's work in *Run*, we are staring down this particular "finish line" of study, and my hope is that this has been for you a joyous and sweet and meaningful couple of miles. But let's not run right past the idea that not all finish lines are celebratory. Sometimes we Run the long slog of a particular Race, only to find ...

- the pink slip is handed to us ...
- the words "I want a divorce" are spoken to us ...
- a friendship has fizzled and feelings are hurt ...
- the biopsy came back positive ... again ...
- straight out of rehab, the child heads back to the drug ...
- just when you thought you were in the clear financially, you need a new transmission ...
- we get the middle-of-the-night call to tell us a loved one has passed ...

Has there been a situation in your life (either now or in the past) when the ending of something felt more like a tragedy than a victory?

Do you know who specializes in turning tragedies into victories? That would be the One who, literally, crossed the Finish Line of all finish lines and declared:

It. Is. *Finished.*

What did Christ Jesus finish on the cross? He conquered death. He conquered sin. He made a way. He redeemed everything you are going through and added buckets and buckets of sweetness and richness to the joys of your life!

Jesus won the victory *for you* on the cross, and if we allow Him to, Jesus will win the victory in our lives as well. What does your Race look like today?

If you are consumed with grief, remember that *Jesus bore* your *grief.*

If you are overwhelmed with sorrows, remember that *He carried* your *sorrow.*

If you are trapped in a pattern of sin, remember that *Jesus was wounded for* your *transgressions.*

If you are not at peace, remember that *He was chastised for* your *peace.*

If you are sick, remember that *Jesus was bruised for* your *healing.*

Jesus did all this "for the joy that was set before Him." Think about this for a moment ... where is the joy in going to the cross? Where is the joy in dying an excruciating death? Where is the joy in being rejected by people you love? Scorned, scoffed, humiliated?

For Jesus, the joy was in what would happen when He finished His Race: *you* would happen. *You,* knowing Him, loving Him, serving Him, living in victory because of Him ... would happen.

It was all for you.

And Jesus knows something you don't: He knows how your story will *end.* He knows that wherever you are in your Race, you are only in the middle of it! He knows that whatever flavor of mess you find yourself in, there will be a turn where you invite Him again, and of course He will come to you, and the *thing will turn around.*

Or you will come out the other side at peace.

Or the relationship will be healed.

Or you will find inexplicable joy waiting on the biopsy results.

Or the prodigal will come home.

Or the struggle you went through will be used to minister to others to the point that one day you will think, "I would not have chosen that Race, but hallelujah, I am honored to share my story and how Jesus rescued me, and then shout to the world, *'How great is our God.'*"

Are you agreeing with the Father's finished work in your life?

Will you allow the Father to finish His mission through your life?

Are you Running your Race with the Joy set before you?

Offer it up to Him. Offer it *all* up to Him. Jesus sees *right now* what you will look like when you cross all your finish lines and He has lavished upon you His mercy and grace … Oh, won't you let Him?

Now *to Him who is able to do immeasurably more than all we ask or imagine, according to his power that is at work within us, to* Him *be the* Glory *in the church and in* Christ Jesus *through all generations, forever and ever!* AMEN!

SESSION SIX: A WINNER!

Day Five Personal Running Log

Pace yourself

Review the week's work: the scripture you have covered, the writings on the lines and in the margins. What would you ask God for this day? What did you not quite get this week? How can you serve Him more? Who and what should you be praying for?

P Pray.
A Ask for God's vision for your life.
C Communicate back to God.
E Enter His Race for your life.

Run free in the space below: _____

Recovery questions

***What main thing did the study push me to *do*, *be*, or *feel* as a result of the material?

***What did God say to me through this week?

***How is my Run measuring up to these words? What action(s) will I take to bring my life in line with the words/messages received this week?

My challenge

With what truth do I need to study and Train harder?

BLISTER:

"Ouch and Pinch": Jot down those moments this week that caused pain.

BLISS:

"Praise You and Thank You": Jot down your praises.

Team Spirit/Sharing Challenge: Think of someone you know who is limping right now.

Pray for them.
Look for an opportunity to share with them what you have learned this week.

THEME VERSE:

Do you not know that in a race all the runners run, but only one gets the prize? Run in such a way as to get the prize. Everyone who competes in the games goes into strict training. They do it to get a crown that will not last; but we do it to get a crown that will last forever. Therefore, I do not run like a man running aimlessly; I do not fight like a man beating the air. No, I beat my body and make it my slave so that after I have preached to others, I myself will not be disqualified for the prize. (1 Corinthians 9: 24–27)

Write out the verses in the space below.

Pray the verses back to God, making them personal.

When you've memorized them, share *the verses by speaking them out loud to your small group! Great job!*

SESSION SEVEN

1 CORINTHIANS 9: 24–27

Do you not know that in a race all the runners run, but only one gets the prize? Run in such a way as to get the prize. Everyone who competes in the games goes into strict training. They do it to get a crown that will not last; but we do it to get a crown that will last forever. Therefore, I do not run like a man running aimlessly; I do not fight like a man beating the air. No, I beat my body and make it my slave so that after I have preached to others, I myself will not be disqualified for the prize.

SESSION SEVEN: LECTURE NOTES

PRAYING THE LANES

A track has eight lanes, and on a typical track-training day for me, you
will find that I have named them. I started doing this six years ago –
many a morning or evening, you will find me in a lane, running …

But what is running through my mind?

Below I will share a secret that has me Running toward the
Mark with expectation and perseverance. As I run physically,
I have assigned myself a spiritual task on that particular lap. I
have outlined my general pattern below, but I do occasionally
change it up, depending on what is going on in my life.

LANE ONE is always where I start. This Lane is all
about God and me and the Race He has called me
to. The verse I pray out loud is Psalm 25:4–5.

*"Show me Your ways, O Lord, and teach me Your paths. Guide me in Your Truth
and teach me, for You are God my Savior and my hope is in You all day long."*

But when I pray it, I personalize it, like this: "Show me my
Race, Lord – is it 'this' You would have me do?" "Teach me
to Run in Your truth in that season or on a specific mile …"
"Thank You for Your salvation … I acknowledge Who You
are." "I confess my sin, weaknesses, and struggles …"

LANE TWO is always family. In this lane, I pray for my husband
first, and then each child in birth order. Each time I go to
another person, I change the lane. So this praying I do in Lanes

two through five. This is how I pray for each family member. It is very powerful, and the backbone of many of my prayers. Remember that God says we are being changed from glory to glory, and through faith you and your loved ones will get there.

In Leviticus 14, the Bible speaks of how the priest goes outside the camp and takes the blood, dips hyssop in the blood and sprinkles the leper seven times. The priest applied the blood to the leper's *ear, thumb,* and *toe.*

Hang with me here! I explain this because I actually and literally pray the covering of the Blood of Jesus Christ over myself and my family's body parts as I walk the track! Anointing comes from the Blood!

So my prayer over each member looks like this:

EAR = Thought life. I pray for their mind and for Christ to find His way into their day. We hear things all day long, and what we hear affects our thinking, so I visually place the Blood on their ear: "Lord, I pray the Blood of the Lord over my husband's ear."

THUMB = Work life. I pray the Blood of Jesus over their talents, gifts, and futures; for God to bring favor to whatever they touch. Romans 11:29: *"For God's gifts and His call are irrevocable."*

TOE = Everyday walk life. I pray over their paths and the people and places they will travel. I pray God works all for the good.

The Bible says we are sanctified and set apart by the Blood (1 Peter 1:2), so I pray the Blood over their lives, and I've also been known to touch their toes and ear lobes in the middle of the night while they are sleeping.

PSALM 1:1–3: "Blessed is the man who does not walk in the counsel of the wicked or stand in the way of sinners or sit in the seat of mockers. But his delight is in the law of the Lord and on his law he meditates day and night. He is like a tree planted by streams of water which yields its fruit in season and whose leaf does not wither. Whatever he does prospers."

LANE SIX is for Leadership. This is for the leaders of the world and of my church. (Psalm 78:72)

LANE SEVEN is my prayers for others. This is for those in my life who have asked for prayer, or have a need I know of. (Thessalonians 5:16–18, Philippians 4:6–7)

LANE EIGHT wraps it up and seals the deal! These are my prayers for God to show me who He would like me to find that day, and to show me how I can encourage and serve and win them for His glory.

As you consider whether to adapt this approach, let me add that it is very flexible.

Instead of lanes, I know people who pray at streets as they drive by … Some have assigned scripture prayers to rooms in their houses … Some do "the hours," in which at the top of each hour, there is a passage or a prayer or a person that they always bring to God.

The Praying Lanes is simply my structure to learn deeper faithfulness and attentiveness. It establishes a regular "appointment" with God and sets the rhythm of my life.

How might God establish a pattern of prayer in your life?

You did it!

At the end of every footrace, the runners are so excited to cross the finish line, of course, but can we talk about the medals? Who doesn't like to wear *that* to the grocery store, just in case someone would ask why they are wearing it?

My very first 10K finish is burned into my memory. I was a nervous runner, and I was a very S-L-O-W runner. In fact, by the time I got to the end – elated – I was told they had *run out of medals*. It seems that in planning for the right number of medals in these kinds of races, organizers only account for the people who actually register for the race and pay to participate. But then on race day, interlopers show up – without having registered or paid. Because they were faster than me, one of them got the medal that should have come to me.

I had worked so hard.

I cried until my face was all puffy, and even though my husband gave me his medal, it just wasn't the same, you know? I had done the work – followed the rules – and been cheated.

How many of us labor invisibly? How often has the fruit of our labors gone to someone else? Yeah. Enough to sting in the remembering, right?

Here's the beauty of knowing Jesus. He sees all. You are never invisible to Him. Your reward – and mine – is not only coming for sure … a nice chunk of it is already here! We get to do life with the Creator of the universe, with whom we are on a first-name basis. *Jesus.* Oh, that is sweet on the tongue. And then we get to live in His *joy* for all time.

This *Run* Race ends well. It is complete, and it is a dream come true for me. And it's not over …

Just before our theme scripture verse, in 1 Corinthians 9:19–23, we find Paul's aim in this whole passage.

"Though I am free and belong to no man, I make myself a slave to everyone to win as many as possible. To the Jews I became like a Jew, to win the Jews. To those under the law I became like one under the law (though I myself am not under the law), so as to win those under the law. To those not having the law I became like one not having the law (though I am not free from God's law, but am under Christ's law), so as to win those not having the law. To the weak I became weak, to win the weak. I have become all things to all men so that by all possible means I might save some. I do all this for the sake of the gospel, that I may share in its blessings."

Paul's aim was to use his new freedom and access within the sphere of influence he had to *win* others to Christ. Five times in this passage Paul expresses ...

"that I might win *as many as possible ..."*
"that I might win *the Jews ..."*
"that I might win *those under the law ..."*
"that I might win *those without law ..."*
"that I might win *the weak ..."*

As I was running one morning I found myself thanking God for the freedom to run. Bold as this may sound, I am not at all deserving: my legs should be cut off. I know this is vivid ... but what came over me was that given all that I had been through and done in my life, I didn't deserve legs! And yet on that morning run, I was overcome with gratitude in the realization that God had come to me, called my name and said, "You are Mine and I love you. Here are your new limbs. Now, put one foot in front of the other and My Spirit will show you how to Run."

But for God.

1 Thessalonians 5:9 reminds us that God did not appoint us to suffer wrath, but to receive salvation through our Lord Jesus Christ.

So I'm sporting some new legs these days. God did that. The freedom to physically and spiritually run free has never been so invigorating to me. For Love's sake, I have shared pieces of my story so that I may win others, and encourage, exhort, and admonish them to:

Run.

In.

Such.

A.

Way!

Lord, grant us Your favor, that we might fully realize our undeserved freedom to become servants to all, that we might win *some.*

Thank you for Running with me these weeks. Now, Friends ... go Run for the glory of God! That's the true win!

Heather